John Ruskin, Augusta Mary Wakefield

Ruskin on music

John Ruskin, Augusta Mary Wakefield

Ruskin on music

ISBN/EAN: 9783337084707

Printed in Europe, USA, Canada, Australia, Japan

Cover: Foto ©Thomas Meinert / pixelio.de

More available books at **www.hansebooks.com**

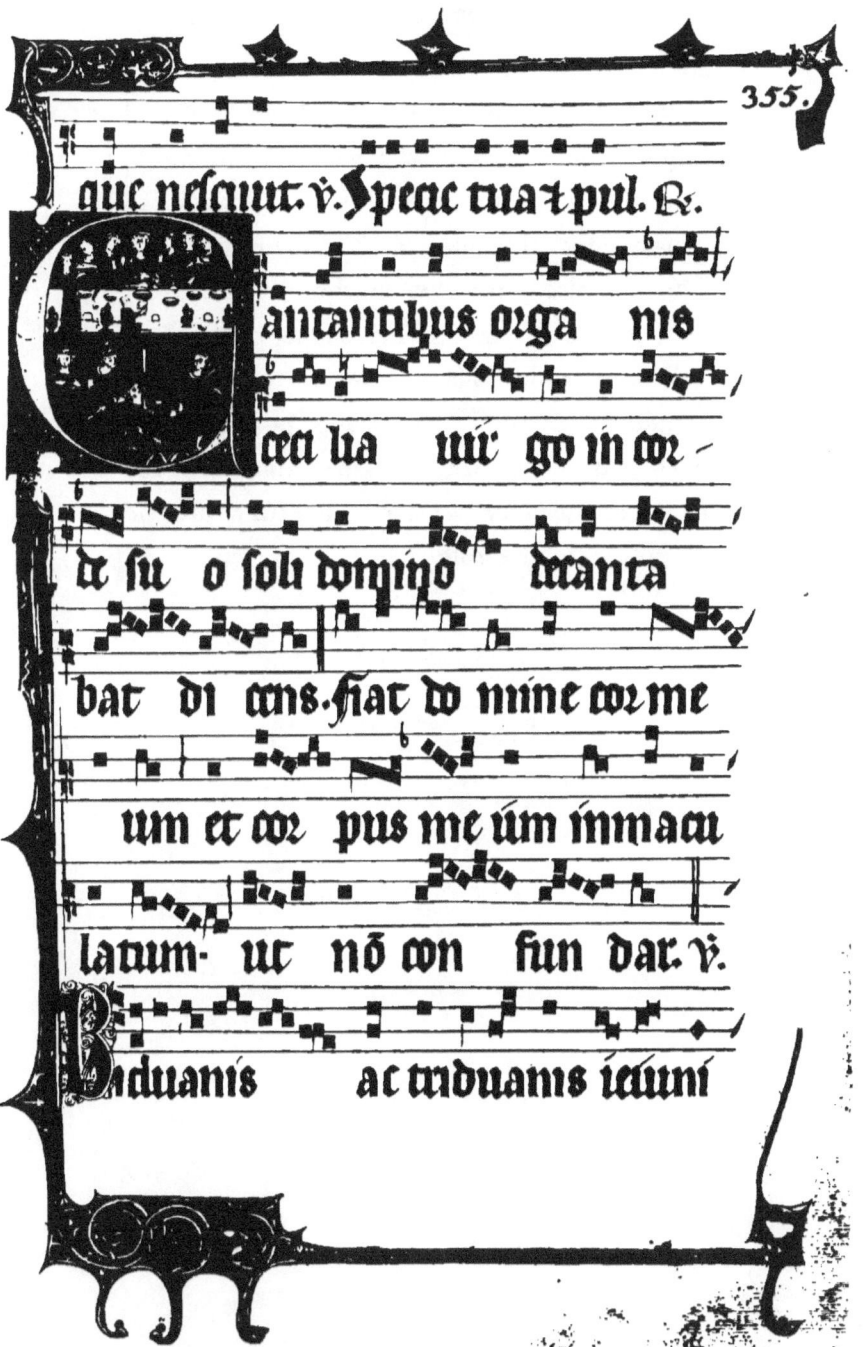

MINIATURE OF ST CECILIA.
From an Antiphonaire of 1290 which belonged to the Abbesse of Beau Pré
Size of original 19 in. X 13 in. See page 136.

PREFACE

THE following extracts have been gathered together merely with the view of putting in collective form the thoughts of "Ruskin on Music" for the use of his many students who are also interested in the Art of Music; and who, accustomed to his manner of teaching, will look behind his words for the thoughts contained therein. To make people think, ever has been Mr. Ruskin's aim, and the passages he has written on Music are no exception to the rule.

CONTENTS

Frontispiece—FACSIMILE IN COLOUR OF LEAF FROM ANTIPHONAIRE OF XIII. CENTURY

See pages 136 *and* 138

CHAP.		PAGE
I.	INTRODUCTION—OF THE IDEAL IN MUSIC	1
II.	MUSIC AND EARLY INFLUENCES	9
III.	MUSIC AND PAINTING	37
IV.	MUSIC AND EDUCATION	68
V.	MUSIC AND MORALS	112
VI.	CONCLUSION—OF MUSIC AND "JOANNA'S CARE"	142

CHAPTER I.

INTRODUCTION.

OF THE IDEAL IN MUSIC.

"The great purpose of Music, which is to say a thing that you mean deeply, in the strongest and clearest possible way."—*Fors*, ix. 15.

WHEN a man is the possessor of world-wide fame in one special line, it often happens that some points in his work—interesting in themselves—are eclipsed by the lustre of the main theme, and remain overlooked by many ardent students of his writings, who, perhaps, belong, as a rule, to the one class to which these writings first and specially appeal. These, in Mr. Ruskin's case, of course, are, first of all, the great brotherhood belonging to the arts of Painting, Drawing, and Architecture. At the same time, even the lesser thoughts of a great thinker contain much that is valuable for those who care to study them, and it seems as if those which have been specially interesting to me come with a peculiar freshness and originality from the fact of their *not* being, so to speak, connected with the profession of Ruskin's life, but with its relaxation. Whenever a mind like his touches any subject, it is bound to leave a particular stamp on that subject; and it is on that account as well as for the artistic teaching contained in these by-thoughts of his, that they have seemed to me to be of characteristic interest and value.

The sentence selected as the heading for this chapter may be taken to contain, in little, Ruskin's musical creed, and indeed is the root of everything contained in the following pages. Even taken alone, these few words show perception of, and instruction in, the deepest view of the art of Music. What a revolution in many systems of teaching the realisation of this little sentence, if properly understood, might bring about! Its result would be that, instead of giving endless pupils a certain amount of technical skill, teachers would understand and search for that intellectual and spiritual quality which enables the few "to say a thing you mean deeply in the strongest and clearest possible way" by means of Music. These words express a power which carries those who possess it through every range of human feeling, and enables others to follow them; which has lifted the art of Music from a tinkling of cymbals to a great intellectual force; which, in its highest efforts, has established Music as a universal language of sympathy through the power of Sound.

But alas! in our generation, Music the ideal and Music the practical seem to have agreed in their ordinary rounds to part company—the practical, of course, in the nineteenth century, triumphantly predominating; though there are few of us who, if asked the question, would not answer truthfully enough how greatly they preferred that simplicity in Music in which the expression of the ideas of Love, Joy, or Sorrow has often brought tears to the eyes, to meaningless technical achievements. Must it, then, be forced upon us that this power of "*meaning deeply*" is one of the rarest gifts of the gods?—that it is akin to genius, and that no cultivation can give it? Technical achievements have shouldered it out of sight for long, but it *is* the spirit of Music and of all true art—the power by which Orpheus won souls, which somehow cannot be got into an examination paper, and which hardly seems recognised when it exists. Let us in imagination reverse all this, make the higher ideal and meaning of Music sought for before all in the work of our musical students, and

"The great purpose of Music, which is to say a thing you mean deeply, in the strongest and clearest possible way," may produce

"Regulations which will bring about some curious changes in piano-playing, and several other things!"*

Naturally, this view of Music may be most interesting to those in whom the intellectual perception of Music's power is in advance of their knowledge of its technicalities. It has often excited interest to observe how very distinct from musicianship is the power of intellectual appreciation of Music, proving the enormous value of the *meaning* of Music, when such can exist, for those to whom its simpler and more prominent forms of sound do not appeal. Truly, "Powers there are which touch each other to the quick, in modes which the gross world no sense hath to perceive, no soul to dream of."

In endeavouring to put together what Mr. Ruskin has said to us on the subject of Music,

* " Fors Clavigera," No. ix. p. 15.

I have found that nearly all his appreciative writing regarding it belongs to the work of his later years, though a few words as to its moral power are to be found in the preface to "Modern Painters," vol. i. p. xxiv., written in 1843. In youth Music does not seem to have been an important influence in his life, so it is the more striking that in after life he gives it such full perception and importance. It is easy to see that some vibrating influence must have suddenly caused him to realise the "deep meaning" of Music, and, indeed, it is well known that Music is closely connected with the romance of John Ruskin's life. But, that perception, came in no sense from the result of early training, rather, indeed, in spite of it, is very evident; though at the same time it was impossible, even without a special influence, that a mind like Ruskin's could go through life without an understanding perception of *any* art, and though *full* appreciation of Music only belonged to his later years, he refers to it again and again with almost curious insistency in his early works, as illustrating canons of art. The intangibility of sound had gotten a hold on him which he could not understand, which perplexed and yet fascinated him. These passages are interesting; first, as showing the close connection in Ruskin's mind between two of the arts and how nearly true critical perception of one art is interwoven with that of another, and, secondly, as the words of a master of language and word painting, on a subject that much lacks intellectual expression in treatment. There are not many Robert Schumanns among us, whose writings, along with those of such critics as Hueffer, have the deepest value, combining as they do intellectual and musical criticism. But there are two sides to musical criticism, both equally interesting; the one, which is scientific analysis of musical form and treatment, possible only to experienced musicians, the other, which is the spiritual perception of the æsthetic side and influence of music, possible for any great mind whose perceptions are keenly cultivated in the highest canons of any art. Schumann represented the ideal musical critic, in that both of these essential points in criticism are to be found in his writings. Ruskin, of course, never realised music scientifically or technically at all (and one does not claim for him the position of a musical critic), but this perhaps renders his thorough perception of its spiritual and æsthetic value all the more remarkable, combined as it is with a sort of clairvoyance (for it can only be so named) into the "deeper meaning" which must underlie all true art, and especially the art of Music.

Such then must be the line upon which we approach what Ruskin has written on Music. He has applied the same search for "meaning" to sound, which he did to colour, and as in the blood red colour of some Turner skies, he felt and traced the sorrow or destruction which it always represented, so has he pointed out that the value of musical sound is in proportion to its faithful representation of the underlying, truest, and deepest meanings of the human soul.

CHAPTER II.

MUSIC AND EARLY INFLUENCES.

> "'Hush-a-bye baby, upon the tree-top' my mother used to sing to me: and I remember the dawn of intelligence in which I began to object to the bad rhyme which followed:—'when the wind blows, the cradle will rock.'"—*Fors*, xxiv. 19.

No doubt the early influences of childhood and manhood were, in Ruskin's case, most antagonistic to Music. It is said, indeed, that music and musicians did not enter into Mr. Ruskin *père's* system of education, and that once when, in a moment of youthful enthusiasm, after hearing and meeting Jenny Lind, the son asked leave to invite her to visit the family mansion at Denmark Hill, permission was kindly but firmly refused, an opera singer not belonging to the sort of society that could be received there! Such being the influences surrounding his youth, Ruskin's later insight into Music is the more remarkable, though no doubt when he first turned towards it, and testified his achieved allegiance to the art, it was more that he recognised in it an important element in general education, than from any very great appreciation of the art for its own sake.

He tells in "Præterita,"* however, in what his early musical opportunities consisted, and first, apparently, come the efforts of some amateurs, constant visitors at Denmark Hill. The first sentence on the subject has a sly hit at the character of musicians in general, for we are told that these were* "themselves both good and pleasing musicians (the qualities are not united in all musicians)!"

Ruskin goes on to explain that,

"In this way, from early childhood, I was accustomed to hear a great range of good music completely and rightly ren-

* "Præterita," vol. i. 313.

II. MUSIC AND EARLY INFLUENCES.

dered, without breakings down, missings out, affectations of manner, or vulgar prominence of execution. Had the quartette sung me English glees or Scotch ballads, or British salt water ones, or had any one had gift enough to render higher music with its proper splendour, I might easily have been led to spare some time from my maps and mineralogy for attentive listening. As it was, the scientific German compositions were simply tiresome to me, and the pretty modulations of Italian, which I understood no syllable of, pleasant only as the trills of the blackbirds, who often listened, and expressed their satisfaction by joining in the part songs through the window that opened to the back garden in the spring evening." *

This, however, does not sound like any real attention to Music as an art, and on the same

* "Præterita," vol. i. 318.

page Mr. Ruskin confesses that he did not think he ever heard any masterly professional Music

"until, as good hap was, I heard the best, only to *be* heard during a narrow space in those young days."

In connection with this first great opportunity he writes:

"It puzzles me that I have no recollection of any first sight and hearing of an opera. .... To be taken now at Paris to the feebly dramatic 'Puritani' was no great joy to me; but I then heard, and it will always be a rare, and only once or twice in a century possible, thing to hear, four great musicians (Grisi, Malibran, Mario, Lablache), all rightly to be called of genius, singing together, with sincere desire to assist each other, not eclipse; and to exhibit, not only their own power of singing, but the beauty of the music they sang. . . . ." *

Here we have the dawn of a certain critical attitude towards Music, for Ruskin, though writing many years later, writes of what he felt then, not now. Notwithstanding his hitherto slight attention to Music, he at once grasped three important points in connection with this memorable performance; first, the feebleness of "Puritani" as an opera, which might all the same have easily dazzled an uncritical mind; secondly, he shows keen perception of the beauty of perfect musical execution; and, thirdly, points out of what such perfect execution must always consist, an absolutely faithful rendering of the Music's own beauties, not of each singer's individual effects; a truism, perhaps, but a truism forgotten by ten performers out of twelve.

" Afterwards, a season did not pass without my hearing twice or thrice, at

* "Præterita," vol. i. 319, 320, 321.

least, those four singers; and I learned the better because my ear was never jaded by the intention of the music written for them, or studied by them; and am extremely glad now that I heard *their* renderings of Mozart and Rossini, neither of whom can be now said ever to be heard at all, owing to the detestable quickening of the time. Grisi and Malibran sang at least one-third slower than any modern cantatrice (it is a pretty conceit of musical people to call themselves scientific, when they have not yet fixed their unit of time!); and Patti, the last time I heard her, massacred Zerlina's part in 'La ci darem,' as if the audience and she had but the one object of getting Mozart's air done with, as soon as possible. . . . . Afterwards . . . . I was brought to the point of trying to learn to sing. . . . . In which, though never even getting so far as to read with ease, I nevertheless, between my fine rhythmic ear, and true lover's sentiment, got to understand some principles of musical art, which I shall perhaps be able to enforce with benefit on the musical public mind, even to-day. . . . ." *

The first mention of any genuine musical interest shown in Ruskin's early writings occurs in an unpublished essay, dated 1838, when he would be nineteen years old. Through the kindness of Mrs. Arthur Severn I am able to quote some hitherto unprinted portions of it. It seemed at a first glance as if this essay should wait for the chapter devoted to "Music and Painting," but, on consideration, it will be seen to represent early influences too strongly not to be placed here.

Mr. Collingwood, in his recent "Life of Ruskin," refers to this essay: "Just before the

* "Præterita," vol. i. 322, 323, 324.

summer tour of 1838 to Scotland, John Ruskin was introduced to Miss Charlotte Withers, a young lady who was as fond of Music as he was of Drawing. They discussed their favourite studies with eagerness; and to settle the matter he wrote a long essay on 'The Comparative Advantages of the Studies of Music and Painting,' in which he sets Painting as a means of recreation and of education far above Music." Ruskin also recalls the essay in "Præterita;"* he says, speaking of it:

"We disputed on the relative dignities of Music and Painting; and I wrote an essay nine foolscap pages long, proposing the entire establishment of my own opinions, and the total discomfiture and overthrow of hers, according to my usual manner of paying court to my mistresses. Charlotte Withers, however, thought I did her great honour, and carried away

* "Præterita," vol. i. 409.

II. MUSIC AND EARLY INFLUENCES.

the essay as if it had been a school prize."

The extracts from it have been chosen with special reference to the musical opinions contained in it. The world knows Ruskin's matured views on painting, but these youthful views on music form a curious contrast to opinions expressed later, and are not familiar.

" The power of enjoying Music is like the power of distinguishing tastes in food, a naturally implanted faculty; the power of being gratified by Painting is either the acquired taste of a cultivated mind, or the peculiar gift of an elevated intellect. Brutes can enjoy Music; mice, in particular, are thrown into raptures by it; horses are strongly excited by trumpets, and may be taught to dance in excellent time, or even to beat a tambourine with their fore-feet; the iguana, a kind of lizard, is so passionately fond of music that if you will but do him the favour to whistle to him, even though you should happen to be but a second-rate musician, he will allow [you] to kill him rather than stir. Snakes will dance in time, elephants will perform elegant *pas-seuls;* but I never heard of even that most sagacious animal becoming an admirer of Raphael, or a connoisseur in the works of Correggio; and the compliment of the birds to Zeuxis was a mere mistake, for they would have admired the bunch of grapes much more.* The power, there-

---

* Zeuxis and Parrhasius contended for the prize of Painting. Zeuxis painted a bunch of grapes; the birds came and pecked at the picture, and everybody considered the piece a *chef d'œuvre.* Parrhasius produced a painting, apparently covered with a curtain, which he told Zeuxis to draw, and look at the picture. Zeuxis attempted to do so, and was astonished when he found that the curtain was painted. The prize was unanimously awarded to Parrhasius, because Zeuxis had deceived birds only, but Parrhasius had deceived Zeuxis.

II. MUSIC AND EARLY INFLUENCES. 19

fore, of enjoying Music, being common to brutes, must be considered inferior to the capability of appreciating Painting, which is peculiar to him who was made after the image of God. . . . .

"We will follow up this comparison with instances assigning to Music its utmost power; for in general it is a mere sensual gratification, not even acting on the feelings ;[!] it is only under peculiar circumstances that it operates with its whole power. There are few things that appear to elevate the mind more than fine sacred Music; but this is because it is fine, not because it is sacred. Let a congregation sing a hymn without instruments—although that is hardly fair to poor Music, for they'll be sure to play the deuce with the tune, clerk and all— but let them be supposed to give it in good style, in a little shabby chapel, no echoes, no fine architecture, and in a simple up and down *hew-haw* sort of tune, it will produce no effect upon the hearer. But let a glorious *Te Deum* be thundered from a noble organ into the dim and misty aisles of some vast and shadowy cathedral, the clear voices of the choristers joining at intervals, now low, now loud, until the pure tones echo and roll like the deep billows of a swelling sea among the sculptured columns, and every niche of Gothic tracery is full of sound, the effect of such music upon the mind is astonishing, and at first a person would be ready to believe that the tones were really addressing themselves to his intellect. But this is not the case; for, first, the impression is not all made by the music. The vast aisles, the sculptured columns, the tinted windows, the pale monuments, all add to the sublime

II. MUSIC AND EARLY INFLUENCES.

impression; and, more than all these, the sense of the purpose of the building and the meaning of the music, the awe that is produced by so sublime a worship. . . . .

" Let us observe the effect of Music in other instances, in which, though more simple, it will be found quite as powerful. The shepherds on the high Alps live for months in a perfect solitude, not perhaps seeing the face of a human being for weeks together. Among these men there is a very beautiful custom—the manner in which they celebrate their evening devotions. When the sun is just setting, and the peaks of eternal snow become tinted of a pale but bright rose-colour by his dying beams, the shepherd who is highest upon the mountains takes his horn and sounds through it a few simple but melodious notes, signifying 'Glory be to God!' Far and wide on the pure air floats the sound; the nearest shepherd hears and replies; and from man to man, over the illimitable deserts of a hundred hills, passes on the voice of worship. Then there is a silence, a deep, dead silence; every head is uncovered, every knee bowed; and from the stillness of the solitude rises the voice of supplication heard by God only. Again the highest shepherd sounds through his horn 'Thanks be to God,' again is the sound taken up and passed on from man to man along the mountains. It dies away; the twilight comes dimly down, and every one betakes himself to repose.

"In this custom there is something peculiarly impressive, but it is owing chiefly to concomitant circumstances; and the music of the horn, if it were used for another purpose and in another place, would be heard without any excited feeling. It is the stillness of the solitude, the grandeur of the mountains, the beauty of the twilight, and the simplicity of the worship, which create sensations so sublime in the hearer, which makes so strong an impression on his feelings, and appeal so vividly to his mind.

"Again, in the effect which the air of the 'Ranz des Vaches' produces upon the Swiss we have a striking instance of the power of Music, but it is of music combined with peculiar associations. This air is one with which the very winds of Switzerland are filled; the chamois-hunter sings it aloud as he flashes on his dark and dreadful path; the peasant chants it in the valley among the brown corn; the maiden's clear voice flings it upon the pure air as she wends to the spring of waters; and the child sings the same notes when he is playing among the flowers. What marvel, then, that when the poor exile hears the same air in a far land, the air which made his step firm on the glacier, or his foot light on the village green, which is associated with all the pleasures and the dangers of his childhood and his youth—what marvel that the yearning for the place of his birth, for the land of his love, should come near even unto death. I will grant that nothing but Music could mingle itself so intricately with the heart-strings, and yet, in all these instances, it is not Music alone; it is combined with something of far higher power, and which appeals to far deeper feelings, and arouses infinitely mightier thoughts. We grant that the association could not be raised without the music. But what would the music be without the association? . . . .

"Thus, then, we have seen that, of the different kinds of music, some owe their astonishing power to association, others to concomitant circumstances; but that in all cases it can operate upon the feelings only. Josephine, when Napoleon had exploded into one of his ungovernable furies, was wont to play to him one simple but beautiful air, which always soothed and pacified him. There is no doubt that, as Music can raise violent passions so it can allay them, or produce softer passions in their room; but we cannot tell that much of the power of this air upon the Emperor was not owing to some association with the scenes of his childhood, or some other circumstance, which added to its power. When we allow this mighty and almost irresistible power of exciting the passions or calling up the affections, when we have seen how well it may be employed to stimulate ardour, to favour meditation, or put the mind in a proper temperament for devotion, I think we have said nearly all that can be said in favour of the art of Music in the way of argument, though much may be yet done by high authority. . . . .

"Again, we are told that there will be Music in heaven, but no Painting; but as the persons who tell us so have hitherto never been there, and perhaps are still far enough from it, their authority is not altogether to be depended upon. . . . .

"Lastly, to render perfect the comparison, let us consider the difference between a fine air and a fine painting. The first thing that strikes us is the proportionate time and labour requisite to produce them. The tune may be dashed off by the inspiration of five minutes ; [!] the picture is the result of the labour and thought of months. This, however, is of little importance, for it is not the time occupied, but the thing done which we have to consider. Now, the music pleases the ear, excites the feelings a little; and that is all. The painting, by its harmonious arrangement of colour, and beautiful disposition of light and shade, gratifies the eye as much as the music the ear ; but then, it addresses itself to the mind ; it is a representation of feeling and action of man, or of the beauty and the soul of Nature, and whether one or the other, is a source of mental gratification of the highest kind, a thing which we may look upon day after day and hour after hour with renewed feelings of wonder and delight, a thing in which a story may be told, a lesson taught, an example conveyed, a poem included—nay, even a Deity imagined. What! shall that which has been worshipped by mistaken zeal be degraded and scorned by ignorant indifference? Shall that to which the error of admiration has bowed the knee be neglected by the blindness of imbecility, or depreciated by the malignity of envy? No: let both the arts be admired and encouraged, but let them never be considered as equal; let the musician be honoured, but the painter be revered; and, above all, let his works be preserved and protected as much as in us lies, since, once lost they are lost for ever, and the hand which alone could produce them is now dust and ashes, and the soul which alone could imagine them sleeping in the stillness of the grave."

II. MUSIC AND EARLY INFLUENCES.

In connection with this essay, Mr. Collingwood's synopsis of the whole must be given, and a few words of his deductions from it. First the synopsis:

"To the higher forms of Music he (Ruskin) awards no such power of compelling emotion, and finds no intellectual interest in them to make up for the loss; whereas in painting, the higher the art the stronger the appeal, both to the senses and the intellect. He describes an ideal 'Crucifixion' by Vandyke or Guido, insisting on the complexity of emotions and trains of thought roused by such a picture. He goes into ecstasies over a typical 'Madonna' of Raphael; discusses David's 'Horatii,' and concludes that even in landscape this double office of painting, at once artistic and literary, gives it a supremacy to which Music has no claim. As a practical means of education he finds little difficulty in showing that 'with regard to drawing, the labour and time required is the same (as for Music), but the advantages gained will,' he thinks, ' be found considerably superior. These are four: namely (1) the power of appreciating fine pictures; (2) the agreeable and interesting occupation of many hours; (3) the habit of quick observation, and exquisite perception of the beauties of Nature; and, lastly, the power of amusing and gratifying others.'"

Mr. Collingwood's deductions from the essay are, that "in the examples chosen, we see the boy who admired as yet without full discrimination; in the line of thought taken we see the man. He never was a musician: he learnt to play and sing a little, and he has composed a few pretty little melodies as an amusement of his later years. He takes great delight in ballad singing and in the simpler forms of old operatic music. But he has no ear for the higher efforts of the art; is not what we call musical."

Certainly not from an executive and technical point of view, but that is not sought for here; and, moreover, these views on Music were the views of youth, and must be qualified greatly

II. MUSIC AND EARLY INFLUENCES. 31

by the very apparent jealousy of the young art critic for the art he loved best, though even here is perception of the emotional power of music.

Two years later, in a letter from Rome in 1840, we have a perfect bit of Ruskin's word painting, again showing comprehension of the emotional power of church music (possibly belonging for the most part to the old Italian church school, though Mr. Ruskin might not know it), which argues a certain growing appreciation of the best in Music. He says of it :

"I heard a noble service in one of the parish churches yesterday, and an hour and a half of magnificent organ and chorus—three organs answering each other, and the whole congregation joining—as Italians can do always—in perfect melody; the church, a favourable specimen, one blaze of Oriental alabaster and gold; the altar, with pillars of lapis lazuli running up fifty feet, more than a foot in diameter, at a guinea an inch in mere material, with groups of white marble flying round and above them, and the roof rising in an apparent infinite height of glorious fresco; and every possible power of music used to its fullest extent—the best pieces of melody chosen out of standard operas and every variety of style, exciting, tender, or sublime—given with ceaseless and overwhelming effect, one solo unimaginably perfect, by a chosen voice thrilling through darkness. All music should be heard in obscurity."*

So end those of Ruskin's thoughts about Music which may be attributed to youthful influences. No great appreciation of the value of the art can possibly be argued from them; but no man who

* " Essay on Literature and Letters," p. 67.

wrote our "Fors" motto could, at the same time, have endorsed the views expressed in the essay of 1838; and it seems curious, that one who, later, so felt the depth of Music's power, should at first have been struck by little but its ear-tickling emotionalism. It is perfectly true Ruskin never was a musician: his tunes, his playing, and his singing will have no place here; but what the common herd expresses as "inspired," is what Ruskin would call the "deeper meaning" of Music, and that he understood and deeply valued. Notes and words are its implements, and must have their all-important value, but the deeper meaning *may* be understood by one who practically could not use its implements. In later years Ruskin loved Mozart and Scarlatti, which means a certain classic appreciation, and I, personally, well remember his teaching of the "meaning" of "Voi che sapete" to be great in value to the singer, because it came in *where the notes and the words ended.*

Therefore, it does not seem to me that to

establish the value of Ruskin's thoughts on Music it is necessary to prove—which indeed would be impossible—that he was in any sense a musical critic, in the ordinary acceptation of the term. What is to be admired in what he has said of the art, is the beautiful way in which its spiritual meaning and teaching has been expressed by him, in the short passages which he has devoted to it, and in which no one has ever excelled him,

He tells us in "Modern Painters" that—

" The critical and executive faculties are in great part independent of each other ;"

so that—

" it is nearly as great an absurdity to require of any critic that he should equal in execution even the work which he condemns, as to require of the audience which hisses a piece of vocal music that they should instantly chant it in truer harmony themselves"*

—though critics often take advantage of this fact and executants suffer from it! It is in this critical perception of Music's highest sentiment, which may be found in its simplest forms, that some of Ruskin's words about it touch what is held to be the soul of Music. It is more easy to express this simply by means of an example, for which purpose such a song as "The Land o' the Leal" may be taken. If the singer, intellectually and emotionally, conveys through its means, to its hearers, human longing, human sorrow, human loss, and the belief in a future life, there we have the soul of the Music—not the mere words, not the mere tune, but something far beyond either and infinitely above them. This quality in Music, so entirely its own, and so often absolutely overlooked, Ruskin has touched upon as only such a mind could do, and has told us of its purpose,

* "Modern Painters," vol. iii. p. xiii. pref.

"To say a thing that you mean deeply, in the strongest and clearest possible way."

Only from the standpoint I have endeavoured to explain, can Mr. Ruskin's thoughts on Music meet with a fair comprehension, and again let me state that the position of a musical critic is not claimed for him; the object here, is merely, to put before those who care for them, his thoughts on Music from their varying points of view. But as many of these thoughts certainly are of a critical nature, it is best to say that those persons who want practical, musical criticism, must look for it elsewhere; but for the few who care to think, there is teaching to be gathered from Ruskin's words on Music, and for all there is beautiful expression of the fresh perceptions of a singularly spiritual mind, unbiassed by, nay, unknowing of, schools of musical opinion, but searching always, and finding often, the highest ideal meaning which exists in all true Art.

CHAPTER III.

MUSIC AND PAINTING.

"The sequences of colour are like those of sound, and susceptible of all the complexity and passion of the most accomplished music."

"A great colourist will make even the absence of colour lovely, as the fading of a perfect voice makes silence sacred."—*Two Paths.*

In order to follow Ruskin's thoughts about Music more easily, I have thought it well to classify them to a certain extent; those in connection with painting seem naturally to follow here, giving the first place to the art that claimed and held his greatest lifelong devotion. A commencement must be made with the passages contained in "Modern Painters," which succeed chronologically those from the early essay and letter, from which quotation has already been made.

Throughout the five volumes of "Modern Painters" there are a number of references to Music, proving that, notwithstanding the secondary position which we must conclude it held with Ruskin in his youth, it still had made a distinct mark in his mind. In most of these references, Music is used as the best means of illustrating artistic points, otherwise difficult to express. Such is the passage on "unity of sequence" (in a picture), where he says

"The effect of Variety is best exemplified by the melodies of music, wherein, by the differences of the notes, they are connected with each other in certain pleasant relations."*

A few pages further we find thoughts on proportion, which are again explained by means of their musical equivalents :

* "Modern Painters," vol. ii. p. 52.

III. MUSIC AND PAINTING.

"It is utterly vain to endeavour to reduce this proportion to finite rules, for it is as various as musical melody, and the laws to which it is subject are of the same general kind, so that the determination of right or wrong proportion is as much a matter of feeling and experience as the appreciation of good musical composition, not but that there is a science of both, and principles which may not be infringed, but that within these limits the liberty of invention is infinite."*

Such passages as these, however, though perhaps not *strictly* musical, are of interest, and serve to strengthen the canon that the rules of right feeling in any art are the same for one and all.

The next passage of musical interest is not a mere formal comparison, but may be looked

* "Modern Painters," vol. ii. p. 57.

upon as one of Ruskin's teaching attitudes on Art, including Music; he says:

"The group calling themselves Evangelical ought no longer to render their religion an offence to men of the world by associating it only with the most vulgar forms of Art. It is not necessary that they should admit either Music or Painting into religious service; but, if they admit either the one or the other, let it not be bad Music nor bad Painting: it is certainly in nowise more for Christ's honour that His praise should be sung discordantly, or His miracles painted discreditably, than that His word should be preached ungrammatically." *

If this passage received due attention, a revolution would be effected in some church

---

* "Modern Painters," vol. iii. p. 60.

and chapel singing, where often the sounds are such, that the only possible conclusion is that any howl will do for God!

In the third volume of "Modern Painters" Mr. Ruskin has evidently been greatly struck with the words of de Stendhal, in the passage which ends thus, in speaking of melody: "It has no rules, no art is so utterly deprived of precepts for the production of the beautiful;" to which Ruskin adds "so much the better for it and for us." This, again, in Ruskin's mind is translated (if one may put it so) to be of use to the sister art of painting; he says:

"I trust the time will soon come when melody in painting will be understood, no less than in music, and when people will find that, there also, the great melodists have no rules, and cannot have any, and that there are in this, as in sound, 'no precepts for the production of the beautiful.'"*

* "Modern Painters," vol. iii. p. 89.

Other passages occur throughout "Modern Painters," showing that Ruskin has felt that in certain matters of artistic expression nothing could illustrate his meaning so clearly as various points in Music. Here is one relating to the inconsistencies

" between perception of colour and form, which, I have had to insist upon in other places, is exactly like that between articulation and harmony. We cannot have the richest harmony with the sharpest and most audible articulation of words : yet good singers will articulate clearly ; and the perfect study of the science of Music will conduct to a fine articulation." *

A further passage illustrates the introduction of colour :

" Whatever else should be wrong that

* "Modern Painters," vol. iv. p. 54.

should be right: just as, though the music of a song may not be so essential to its influence as the meaning of the words, yet if the music be given at all, *it* must be right, or its discord will spoil the words; and it would be better, of the two, that the words should be indistinct, than the notes false." *

Such passages, though one may not agree with their views, and though they were designed to illustrate painting, have distinct musical interest.

Later, in the same volume, one of the great rules of all art is forcibly expressed:

"In all the noblest compositions, utmost power is permitted, but only for a short time, or over a small space. . . . . Music must rise to its utmost loudness and fall from it, colour must be graduated to its

* "Modern Painters," vol. iv. p. 55.

extreme brightness, and descend from it." *

The whole theory of artistic climax is here brought before us in a few words, the realisation of which every artist, every musician, be he executant or composer, should ever have before him, and without which, none of the finest effects of any art are attainable or perceptible.

The last quotation concludes those gathered from "Modern Painters."

Throughout the "Stones of Venice" are a few more scattered musical allusions, not all, however, separable from their context, and still not so much used for their intrinsic musical interest in the mind of the writer, as to illustrate, as before, artistic points of drawing and painting. Thus, regarding a design intended to be seen near, he says:

" Remove it to a distance and the connecting delicacies vanish, the energies

* "Modern Painters," vol. iv. p. 276.

alone remain .... there is alike a more palpable effect, the retirement of a band of music, in which the instruments are of very unequal powers, the fluting and fifing expire, the drumming remains." *

Again : " Order in its highest is one of the necessities of Art, just as Time is a necessity of Music." In this last quotation it seems as if Ruskin's lack of musical technicality had led him astray in his comparison, for "order," as applied to the composition of Painting, is equally necessary in the composition of Music; time alone would do badly without it!

An important note occurs in the third volume of the "Stones of Venice," showing that Ruskin's mind had not yet undergone much change in its view of Music from the first passage quoted from the early essay of 1838 ; a sort of jealousy for the art of Painting almost seems to have held him captive to prevent his giving Music

* "Stones of Venice," vol. iii.

its due, though he is unable to help himself partially recognising its true value. Of course the subject embodied in the following quotation is one that, perhaps, will ever be a matter for discussion by the partisans of two great arts; but in this instance it compares somewhat curiously with Ruskin's later utterances, where " the power of sound" is extolled to the utmost degree its worshippers could desire. Here he says:

"Nothing is more wonderful to me than to hear the pleasure of the eye in colour spoken of with disdain as 'sensual,' while people exalt that of the ear in Music. Do they really suppose the eye is a less noble bodily organ than the ear?" .... "I do not mean to depreciate Music; let it be loved and reverenced as is just, only let the delight of the eye be reverenced more. The great power of music over the multitude is owing, not to its being less, but *more* sensual in colour; it is so distinctly and so richly sensual, that it can be idly enjoyed; it is exactly at this point where the lower and the higher pleasures of the senses and imagination are balanced; so that pure and great minds love it for its invention and emotion, lower minds for its sensual power."

Ruskin had also spoken in a letter of 1843 of "a keen eye for colour" as "a faculty far more rare than an ear for music."

But, especially in the former passage, one cannot help feeling that here speaks the art critic, jealous of the supremacy for the art he loves most. It could not be granted for an instant that the power over a multitude, of such a song as "Auld Lang Syne," the National Anthem, or "The girl I left behind me," under certain circumstances, has even so much as a touch of what is ordinarily understood by the word sensual; and yet it is hardly possible to credit a whole crowd with love for their "invention," though perhaps for their "emotion." At any rate, a much higher range of feeling is produced by such airs and appealed to in them, than mere pleasure of the senses. This expression of evidently misunderstood feeling makes one think that Mr. Ruskin, in his retired student life, could not at this time have experienced the effect on a crowd, of simple strains, which he would have been the very first to feel and acknowledge with admiration; as he did, later, in the following passage from "Two Paths," which it is irresistible not to place here for immediate reading after the former one. Comparison has been made between Music and Architecture, and Ruskin goes on to say:

"A well-disposed group of notes in Music will sometimes make you weep and sometimes laugh. You can express the depth of all affections by these dispositions of sound; you can give courage to the soldier, language to the lover, consolation to the mourner, more joy to the joyful, more humility to the devout. Can you do as much by your group of lines? Do you suppose the front of Whitehall, a singularly beautiful one, ever inspires the two Horse Guards, during the hour they sit opposite to it, with military ardour?"*

A delightful victory for Sound had been achieved between the writing of these two passages; a victory partly obtained, it seems to me, by the importance given to Music in education by Plato, partly by the instinctive growth of Ruskin's perception of its powers.

To "Two Paths" we owe another interesting comparison between every touch in a painting and the least important notes in a piece of music.

* "Two Paths," par. 104.

"A misplaced touch may sometimes annihilate the labour of hours. Nor are any of us prepared to understand the work of any great master, till we feel this, and feel it as distinctly as we do the value of arrangement in the notes of music. Take any noble musical air, and you find, on examining it, that not one even of the faintest or shortest notes can be removed without destruction to the whole passage in which it occurs; and that every note in the passage is twenty times more beautiful so introduced, than it would have been if played singly on the instrument. Precisely this degree of arrangement and relation must exist between every touch and line in a great picture. You may consider the whole as a prolonged musical composition: its parts, as separate airs connected in the story; its little bits and fragments of colour and line, as separate passages or bars in melodies; and down to the minutest note of the whole—down to the minutest *touch*—if there is one that can be spared—that one is doing a mischief,"* for "the touch of Titian, Correggio, or Turner, is a far more marvellous piece of nervous action than can be shown in anything but colour, or in the very highest executive expression in Music." †

Mentions of Music, in connection with painting, run through most of Ruskin's works the one illustrative of the other art. The first reference in the "Elements of Drawing" is a funny little comparison between colour and "correct singing," by which, it seems, Mr. Ruskin means singing in tune, the shades of tune being very like the shades of colour.

"If you are singing, and sing false

* "Two Paths," par. 44.   † *Ibid.* 160.

notes, it does not matter how true the words are. If you sing at all, you must sing sweetly; if you colour at all, you must colour rightly."*

Also in "The Elements of Drawing" we have another passage devoted to composition; here Ruskin arrives at its similarity, whether in poetry, painting or music. He says:

"In a well-composed air, no note, however short or low, can be spared, but the least is as necessary as the greatest: no note, however prolonged, is tedious; but the others prepare for, and are benefited by, its duration; no note, however high, is tyrannous; the others prepare for, and are benefited by, its exaltation; no note, however low, is overpowered, the others prepare for, and sympathise with, its humility: and the result is, that each and

* "Elements of Drawing," p. 194.

every note has a value in the position assigned to it, which, by itself, it never possessed, and of which, by separation from the others, it would instantly be deprived." *

Every point in this passage, Ruskin applies equally to poetry and painting, going on to say that the form of

"Composition in the arts should strongly affect every order of mind, however unlearned or thoughtless. Hence the popular delight in musical rhythm and metre, and in simple musical melodies." †

Popular, otherwise uninstructed, delight in musical composition, as in all else, naturally turns to the simplest forms of it, as a child does to the shortest words in the language.

* "Elements of Drawing," p. 240.   † *Ibid.* p. 242.

The law of contrast is also shown to be necessary in Music, though spoken of perhaps a little slightingly as an "artifice perpetual in Music, and perpetual also in good illumination."*

An interesting passage on the law of expression occurs a few pages later in the same book.

Among those are laws which

"I never hope to be able to explain, laws of expression, bearing simply on simple matters; but, for that very reason more influential than any others . . . . it being just as impossible, I think, to explain why one succession of musical notes shall be lofty and pathetic, and such as might have been sung by Casella to Dante, and why another succession is base and ridiculous, and would be fit only for the reasonably good ear of Bottom." †

* "Elements of Drawing," p. 295.   † *Ibid.* pp. 315, 316.

III. MUSIC AND PAINTING.

This matter of expression in certain sounds has also again and again been noted by Ruskin to explain the expression of certain colours; and he says here, speaking of the best arrangement of colour, "we like it, just as we like an old air in Music, but cannot reason any refractory person into liking it" (I think one may add *because*)

"The best part of every great work is always inexplicable: it is good because it is good."*

The next extract refers to the change that might be brought about in public feeling for art under certain conditions; the passage is introduced in connection with some thoughts on the power of design which is so often to be found far apart from real genius.

"The multiplication of designs by painters of second-rate power is no

* "Elements of Drawing," pp. 315, 316.

more desirable than the writing of Music by inferior composers. . . . ."

Ruskin goes on to say that in painting good copies of great masters are better than bad originals, just as

"The rendering of Music by an enthusiastic and highly-trained executant differs from the grinding of a street organ. And the change in the tone of public feeling, produced by familiarity with such work, would soon be no less great than in their musical enjoyment, if having been accustomed only to hear black Christy's, blind fiddlers, and hoarse beggars scrape or howl about their streets, they were permitted daily audience of faithful and gentle orchestral rendering of the work of the highest classical masters." *

* "Ariadne Florentina," App. p. 245.

III. MUSIC AND PAINTING.

Here is right appreciation of classic beauty in Music, and a just if tardy admission that due study is necessary for the appreciation of its highest qualities.

Leaving design we return to Music in connection with colour, in which comparisons Mr. Ruskin has ever been specially happy: part of this passage is one of the most beautiful and happy descriptions of true artistic feeling, and of the born artist.

" Painting is playing on a colour violin seventy times seven stringed, and inventing your tune as you play on it. This is the easy, simple, straightforward business you have to learn. Here is your catgut and your mahogany; better or worse quality of both of course there may be, Cremona tone, and so on . . . . but the primary question is—*Can* you *play?* Perfectly you never can but by birth gift. The entirely first-rate musicians and painters are born; like Mercury, their words are music, and their touch is gold; sound and colour wait on them from their youth, and no practice will ever enable other human creatures to do anything like them. .... But the matter must still depend on practice *as well as* on genius .... your care as a student, on the whole, is not to be given to the quality of your piano, but of your touch. This is the great fact which I have to teach you respecting colour; this is the root of all excellent doing and perceiving. .... How divine the law of Nature is, which has so connected the immortality of beauty with patience of industry!"*

The one passage concerning Music from the "Seven Lamps of Architecture" is an excellent comparison between proportion and melody.

* "Laws of Fesolé," p. 117.

III. MUSIC AND PAINTING.

"Proportions are as infinite (and that in all kinds of things, as severally in colours, lines, shades, lights, and forms) as possible airs in Music: and it is just as rational an attempt to teach a young architect how to proportion truly and well by calculating for him the proportions of fine works, as it would be to teach him to compose melodies by calculating the mathematical relations of the notes in Beethoven's 'Adelaide' or Mozart's 'Requiem.'"*

It may be doubted whether the following quotation should not find a place in "Music and Morals," but as its real subject is Music and Colour, it is included here.

"The whole science of æsthetics is, in the depth of it, expressed by one passage of Goëthe's in the end of the second part

* "Seven Lamps," pp. 124, 5.

of "Faust;"—the notable one that follows the song of the Lemures, when the angels enter to dispute with the Fiends for the soul of Faust. They enter singing 'Pardon to sinners, and life to the dust.' Mephistopheles hears them first and explains to his troop: 'Discord I hear, and filthy jingling'—'Mistöne höre ich; garstiges Geklimper.' This, you see, is the extreme of bad taste in Music. . . . . Both Music and Colour are naturally influences of peace; but in the war trumpet, and the war shield, in the battle song and battle standard, they have concentrated, by beautiful imagination, the cruel passions of men."*

What Ruskin has written on Music and Painting may be appropriately concluded with his beautiful description of one of the frescoes

* "Aratra Pentelici," pp. 14, 15.

III. MUSIC AND PAINTING. 61

in Santa Maria Novella, Florence. Here both Painting and Music are searched through and through for their powers of deep meaning. The fresco consists of Simon Memmi's figure representing "Music," following that of "Reason."

"After learning to reason, you will learn to sing; for you will want to. There is so much reason for singing in this sweet world, when one thinks rightly of it. None for grumbling, provided always you *have* entered in at the strait gate. You will sing all along the road then, in a little while, in a manner pleasant for people to hear."

"This figure has been one of the loveliest in the series, an extreme refinement and tender severity being aimed at throughout. She is crowned, not with laurel, but with small leaves—I am not sure what they are, being too much injured—the face thin, abstracted and wistful; the lips not far open in their low singing; the hair rippling softly on the shoulders. She plays on a small organ, richly ornamented with Gothic tracery, the slope of it set with crockets like those of Santa Maria del Fiore. Simon Memmi means that *all* music must be 'sacred.' Not that you are never to sing anything but hymns; but that whatever is rightly called Music, or work of the Muses, is divine in help and healing.

"The actions of both hands are singularly sweet. The right is one of the loveliest things I ever saw done in painting. She is keeping down one note only, with her third finger, seen under the raised fourth: the thumb, just passing under; all the curves of the fingers exquisite, and the pale light and shade of the rosy flesh relieved against the ivory white and brown of the notes. Only the thumb and end of the forefinger are seen of the left hand, but they indicate enough its light pressure on the bellows. Fortunately, all these portions of the fresco are absolutely intact.

"Underneath, Tubal-Cain. Not Jubal as you would expect. Jubal is the inventor of musical instruments. Tubal-Cain, thought the old Florentines, invented harmony itself. They, the best smiths in the world, knew the differences in tones of hammer strokes on anvil. Curiously enough the only piece of true part singing, done beautifully and joyfully, which I have heard this year (1874) in Italy (being south of Alps exactly six months and ranging from Genoa to Palermo) was out of a busy smithy at

Perugia. Of bestial howling, and entirely frantic vomiting up of hopelessly damned souls through their still carnal throats, I have heard more than, please God, I will ever endure the hearing of again, in one of His summers.

You think Tubal-Cain very ugly? Yes, much like a shaggy baboon: not accidentally, but with most scientific understanding of baboon character. Men must have looked like that before they had invented Harmony, or felt that one note differed from another, says Simon Memmi. Darwinism, like all widely popular and widely mischievous fallacies, has many a curious gleam and grain of Truth in its tissue.

Under Moses.

Medallion, a youth drinking. Otherwise, you might have thought only church music meant, not feast music also." *

Such are the thoughts of Ruskin, linking together, by laws applicable to both, the arts of Painting and Music. He has given us in these passages the laws of contrast, the laws of composition, the laws of expression, the laws of design, the laws of power, and the laws of colour. All these laws, as applied to Painting, he has illustrated by means of musical description, the terms belonging to which having served better to convey his meaning, than those terms which belong to the art itself. Nearly every illustration has, at the same time, intrinsic, musical meaning. The passages have, in many instances, a wider value than that of comparative illustrations, though interesting as such. Many a word of musical truth is here; many a suggestion of artistic thought is given, of equal value to the painter and the musician, save, in that the musician is poorer than the painter in

* "The Strait Gate," p. 134.

writings which touch the ideal side of his art, so that, therefore, perhaps, the value of such suggestions is greater to him. Throughout all these passages, we see that the strength of Ruskin's words on all art subjects, and their greatest value, is, that he has never lowered any branch of it to an amusement, never allowed it other than a serious signification in life, if we except the views contained in the early Essay of 1838. Music has, of all the arts, been most often lowered to the position of an amusement, notwithstanding many a noble record; therefore, all serious views of it are of special value, bearing in mind that

"The first great principle we have to hold by in dealing with the matter is, that the end of Art is not to *amuse;* and that all Art which proposes amusement as its end, or which is sought for that end, must be of an inferior, and is probably of a harmful class.

The end of Art is as serious as that of other beautiful things—of the blue sky, and the green grass, and the clouds, and the dew. They are either useless, or they are of much deeper function than giving amusement." *

* "Cestus of Aglaia VIII.," p. 528.

CHAPTER IV.

MUSIC AND EDUCATION.

"Every well-trained youth and girl ought to be taught the elements of Drawing, as of Music, early and accurately."—*Laws of Fesolé.**

IN entering upon the portions of Mr. Ruskin's writings which seem to come more immediately under this heading, it is necessary to note how largely his views, and even the manner of expressing them, were influenced by the well-known sayings of Plato relating to Music contained in the "Laws" and the "Republic." I say "well-known," but it is possible that to many of those who are not classical students, Ruskin's fugitive extracts of portions of these Dialogues

* "Laws of Fesolé," pref. p. vi.

may stand as an introduction to ancient classic thought on Music. For this reason his quotations from Plato are included here, though, indeed, it would have been difficult to separate the subject-matter from his comments, so interwoven are they. It should, perhaps, also have been stated sooner that many musical terms used by Ruskin, are evidently used in the sense of their exact translation from the Greek, not by any means as they are now more technically understood in Music. Thus, he often uses the word "harmony," as taken to mean any harmonious sound (not in its ordinarily accepted signification, of a combination of sounds, which Greek Music did not contain). The Platonic view of the use of Music is, without doubt (admitting modifications of it), Ruskin's own view of the Art as an Educator; the passages from Plato, and Ruskin's comments on them, in connection with the subject of Education, shall, therefore, stand first, to be followed in natural sequence of idea, with the musical portion of the latter's sketch of "Ideal England," framing together, a not unimportant educational, musical code, from the point of view of its higher meaning.

The musical teaching of Plato was produced in " Fors," in answer to a Manchester correspondent, who wished to make the art again a teacher, and who wrote saying that Music is one of the things most needed by working people—" good Music, not that which is to be heard in Music-halls,"* to which Mr. Ruskin answers :

" I will take up this subject at length, with Plato's help, in next ' Fors.' Meantime, may I briefly ask if it would not be possible, instead of keeping merely the bad *music* out of the Hall, to keep the bad *men* out of it? Suppose the Music, instead of being charged twopence for, were given of pure grace ; suppose, for instance, that rich people, who now endeavour to preserve memory of their respected

* Correspondence to " Fors Clavigera," No. lxxxi. p. 281.

relations by shutting the light out of their church windows with the worst glass that ever good sand was spoiled into—would bequeath an annual sum to play a memorial tune of a celestial character?—or in any other pious way share some of their own operatic and other musical luxury with the poor; or even appoint a Christian lady visitor, with a voice, to sing to them instead of preach?— Would not the selection of the pieces become easier under such conditions?"*

However, after offering these suggestions, Ruskin faithfully keeps his promise, and takes up in the following "Fors" the subject of Music as treated by Plato, commencing with the statement that:

"To-day, instead of merely using Plato's help in talking of Music, I shall give little more than his own

* "Fors Clavigera" No. lxxxi. p. 282, note *e*.

words, only adding such notes as are necessary for their application to modern needs." *

A Greek gentleman's education, then, which in some modified degree St. George proposes to make universal for Englishmen who really deserve to have it, consisted essentially in perfect discipline in music, poetry, and military exercises. Then came the question, as to what view of these arts was really the highest? with the answer that

"Only brightness of heart can please the gods. . . . . The extreme importance of this teaching is in its opposition to the general Greek instinct, that tragedy or song in honour of the gods should be sad." †

Next follows an interesting note showing the effect on Ruskin's mind of this thought. He says:

* "Fors Clavigera," No. lxxxii. p. 301.
† *Ibid.* pp. 310, 311.

IV. MUSIC AND EDUCATION.

" I thought to have collected into this place the passages about the demoralising effect of sad music (Verdi's, for instance, the most corrupting type hitherto known) [!] from the 'Republic' as well as the 'Laws;' but that must be for next month."

Then comes the account of Plato's division of education for a boy, which ended at sixteen.* The ten years of childhood exclusively to forming the disposition, then three years of grammar, with the collateral sciences, *and then three years' practice in executive music.* For these three years literary study is to be foregone, even by those who are to take it up again, that they may learn Music completely. Upon this Ruskin comments as follows:

"Understanding thus much, we can now clearly understand, whether we receive it or not, Plato's distinct assertion that, as

* "Fors Clavigera," No. lxxxii. p. 311.

gymnastic exercise is necessary to keep the body healthy, 'musical exercise is necessary to keep the soul healthy; and that the proper nourishment of the intellect and passions can no more take place without Music, than the proper functions of the stomach and the blood without exercise."

Strange change of feeling from some passages already quoted!

"We may be little disposed at first, to believe this, because we are unaware, in the first place, how much Music, from the nurse's song to the military band and the lover's ballad, does really modify existing civilised life; and, in the second place, we are not aware how much higher range, if rightly practical, its influence would reach, of which right practice, I must say, before going on with Plato's teaching, that the chief condition is companionship, or choral association (not so much marked by Plato in words, because he could not conceive of Music practised otherwise), and that for persons incapable of song, to be content in amusement by a professional singer, is as much a sign of decay in the virtue and use of Music, as crowded spectators in the amphitheatre sitting to be amused by gladiators are a sign of decline in the virtue and use of war."*

Then again follows Plato's teaching, which Ruskin chose for the ideal in Music, for St. George's Guild, and upon which he has framed his own:

" I say, then, there should be three choirs to fill, as with enchantment of singing, the souls of children while they

* "Fors Clavigera," No. lxxxii. pp. 317, 318.

are tender, teaching them many other things, of which we have told and shall tell, but this chiefly, and for the head and sum of all, that the life which is the noblest is also deemed by the gods the happiest— .... the entire city singing to itself—should never pause in repeating such good lessons as we have explained, yet somehow changing, and so enlaying and varying them, that the singers may always be longing to sing, and delighting in it.*

The three choirs thus referred to are the Choir of the Muses, that of children, up to the age of sixteen;

"after that the Choir of Apollo, formed of those who have perfectly learned the mastery of the lyre—from sixteen to thirty; and then the Choir of Dionysus,

* "Fors Clavigera," No. lxxxii. p. 321.

of the older men, from thirty to sixty; and after sixty, being no longer able to sing, they should become mythologists, relating in divine tradition the moral truths they formerly had sung."

"At this point, if not long before"— Ruskin continues—

"I imagine my reader stopping, hopelessly, feeling the supreme uselessness of such a conception as this, in modern times, and its utter contrariness to everything taught as practical among us. 'Belief in gods, belief in tradition of Myths! Old men, as a class, to become mythologists instead of misers! And Music, throughout life, to be the safeguard of morality! What futility to talk of such things *now*.'"

Notwithstanding the "futility" of this scheme, which does indeed read like a dream of some Goddess of Song, Mr. Ruskin believes sufficiently in its vital principle to continue his researches in Plato for the benefit of his readers in his next letter in " Fors Clavigera."

In reading and thinking over the Platonic scheme, or, indeed, over Ruskin's comments on it, of course it is impossible we should be concerned with the "letter of the law" so to speak; but do they not in either case open suggestions to us of high possibilities of song, of its influences, so apt to be forgotten? Do they not remind us of its time-worn services, not only to art, but to religion, war, teaching, triumph? No art has held such personal connection with every human emotion as Music, and therefore has it the speaking force of a personality, in which lies its greatest strength.

But to return to Plato as given in the next " Fors."

" We said, then, that the sixty years old singers in the service of Dionysus should be, beyond other men, gifted with fine sense of rhythm, and of the meetings together of harmonies; so that being able to choose out of imitative melody, what is well and ill represented of the soul in its passion, and well discerning the picture of the evil spirit from the picture of the good, they may cast away that which has in it the likeness of evil, and bring forward into the midst that which has the likeness of good; and hymn and sing *that* into the souls of the young, calling them forth to pursue the possession of virtue, by means of likenesses. And for this reason the sounds of the lyre ought to be used for the sake of clearness in the chords; the master and pupil keeping both their voices in one note together with the chord: but the changes of the voice and variety of the lyre, the chords giving one tune and the poet another melody, and the oppositions of many notes to few, and of slow to swift, sometimes in symphony, sometimes in antiphony, the rhythm of the song also in every sort of complication inlaying itself among the sounds of the lyre—with all this the pupils who have to learn what is useful in Music in only three years, must have nothing to do: for things opposed, confusing each other, are difficult to learn; and youth, as far as possible, should be set at ease in learning." (Plato.)

Ruskin continues:

"I think this passage alone may show the reader that the Greeks knew more of Music than modern orchestral fiddlers fancy. For the essential work of Stradiuarius, in substituting the violin for the lyre and harp, was twofold. Thenceforward (a) instrumental music became the captain instead of the servant of the voice; and (b) skill of instrumental music, as so developed, became impossible in the ordinary education of a gentleman. So that, since his time, old King Cole has called for his fiddlers three, and Squire Western sent Sophia to the harpsichord when he was drunk: but of souls won by Orpheus, or cities built by Amphion, we hear no more."*

Mr. Ruskin has ever been a warm upholder of the powers of the human voice, and perhaps in these days, when it is treated as a secondary consideration (the natural reaction from its having held an absurd value), it may not be amiss to remember that the one, as a branch of Music, is the gift of God, the other, merely the result of man's cultivation of Art. So important was the teaching of the voice looked upon by ancient writers, that there is, says Mr. Ruskin,

* "Fors Clavigera," No. lxxxiii. pp. 345, 346.

"scarcely a word in Greek social philosophy which has not reference to musical law, and scarcely a word in Greek musical science which has not understood reference to social law."

Plato continues, in final definition:

"The whole Choreia is whole child-education for us, consisting, as we have seen, in the rhythms and harmonies which belong to sound (for as there is a rhythm in the movement of the body, so there is a rhythm in the movement of sound, and the movement of sound we call tune). And *the movement of sound, so as to reach the soul for the education of it in virtue* (we know not how), we call Music."

"You see from this important passage that the Greeks only called 'Music' the kind of sound which induced right moral feeling (they knew not how, but they knew it *did*,) and any other kind of sound than that, however beautiful to the ear or scientific in composition, they did not call 'Music' (exercise under the Muses) but 'Amusia'—the denial, or desolation for want, of the Muses. . . . . The proper word for the opposed delightful art would have been sirenic,"

as an instance of which, Mr. Ruskin speaks of

"the oratorio, withering the life of religion into dead bones on the Syren sands;"

a sentence which has just a shade of truth, in its exaggeration.

" But that we may get rid at once of the need of speaking of such things, shall we not accept for the mould and seal of all song, Euphemy, the speaking the good of all things, and not Blasphemy, the speaking of their sorrow?

"Which first law of noble song is

taught us by the myth that Euphemy was the nurse of the Muses."*

I have placed first, though it occurred in a much later letter in "Fors" than its context, all this thought, which sprung from his study of Plato on "Music, as an educator." It certainly must have been the root of the musical part of Ruskin's sketch of "Ideal England" which, however, follows it. The music for "Ideal England" is valuable as intellectual recognition of the educating influences of the art; not wholly a dreamer's sketch either, though, perchance a little, that of an enthusiastic idealist. But where should we be if the world were bereft of its idealists? They are few enough.

A curious little link between "Plato" and "Ideal England," showing always the bent of Ruskin's mind on Music, may be supplied, in passing (from "Val d'Arno"), as to the importance of musical education in thirteenth century Italy. He says:

* "Fors Clavigera," No. lxxxiii. pp. 349, 350, 362.

"Though a good knight held his education to be imperfect unless he could write a sonnet or sing it, he did not esteem his castle to be at the mercy of the 'editor' of a manuscript. He might indeed owe his life to the fidelity of a minstrel, or be guided in his policy by the wit of a clown; but he was not the slave of venial music or vulgar literature." *

The sketch of Music's part, in "Ideal England," occurs in the fifth letter of "Fors Clavigera," written in May 1871 on the twenty-first page, this letter being preceded by the significant picture of Giotto's "Hope," from the chapel of the Arena at Padua. In this sketch Music is allowed the utmost importance educationally.

"We will have some music and poetry; the children shall learn to dance to

* "Val d'Arno," sec. 88.

it, and sing it—perhaps some of the old people, in time, may also—that is to say, when the various demons of England have allowed them leisure, and [according to Ruskin] the right spirit for song and dance." *

Even in these few words we find the hint developed, of " meaning deeply " in song.

Mr. Ruskin was never left long without having the opportunity of correction for his theories! and in the very next " Fors," we find him brought to book, by a Birmingham correspondent, who reminds him that even his musical instruments must be constructed by the demons of steam, which he always so forcibly denounced ; to which Ruskin

"ventured to answer that porcelain had been painted before the time of James Watt; that even Music was not a recent invention ; that my poor company (the

* "Fors Clavigera," No. v. p. 21.

inhabitants of 'Ideal England') would deserve no better colours than Apelles and Titian made shift with, or even the Chinese; and that I could not find any notice of musical instruments in the time of David, for instance, having been made by steam.*

"To this my correspondent again replied that he supposed David's 'twangling upon the harp' would have been unsatisfactory to modern taste."

Ruskin concludes:

"We shall have to be content, however, for our part (in 'Ideal England') with a little 'twangling' on such roughly made harps as the Jews and Greeks got their melody out of."

Here again we are reminded how triumphantly, in classic times, the ideal beauty must have preponderated; "the spirit of the song"

* "Fors Clavigera," No. vi. pp. 7, 8.

was the question, and represented the influence of Music; and, verily, perfect sound is as nought without it.

Taking the passages in order of date, we come next to the beautiful one relating to the ideal education of children, from which a few words, already quoted, have been extracted.

"On every day, part of their morning service shall be a song in honour of the hero whose birthday it is: and part of their evening service, a song of triumph for the fair death of one whose death-day it is: *and in their first learning of notes they shall be taught the great purpose of Music, which is to say a thing that you mean deeply, in the strongest and clearest possible way; and they shall never be taught to sing what they don't mean.* They shall be able to sing merrily when they are happy, and earnestly when they are sad; but they shall find no mirth in mockery, or obscenity, neither shall they waste and profane their hearts with artificial and lascivious sorrow."*

Much is to be learnt here if one searches a little beyond the words into the real meaning of this passage. It sweeps away the artificial with a strong hand, and it places Truth in Music in the highest place from the "first learning of notes;" it shows that in song high and true sentiment, alike of melody and idea, and in instrumental music, classic beauty in elaborated form, combined with ideal sentiment, should be the true ambition of the musician.

So—and so only—is the "strongest and clearest possible way" attainable.

Next to Music's position in "Ideal England" follow the rules for its pursuit, as laid down for the benefit of St. George's Guild, in "Rock Honeycomb," having for inspiration a strange

* "Fors Clavigera," No. ix. p. 15.

medley, consisting of the Coniston village band and Sir Philip Sidney's divine Psalmody!

But let the laws speak for themselves:

" Yesterday evening, one of the sweetest and brightest of this hitherto sweet summer, the 'Coniston Band,' consisting of the musically minded workingmen of the village, rowed itself for its Saturday at e'en delectation, into the middle of the lake; and floating just between Brantwood and the 'Hall' on the opposite shore—where Sir Philip Sidney, it is delivered by tradition, lived for a time, with his sister, in our Arcadia of western meres—poured forth divers pipings and trumpetings, with meritorious endeavour, and I doubt not real, innocent, and useful pleasure to itself, and to the village hearers on the opposite green shore.

"Mostly, polka music with occasional sublimities—'My Maryland' and 'God save the Emperor!' and the like; pleasant enough, sometimes, to hear from this shore also; but as it chanced yesterday, very destructive of my comfort in showing the bright roses and deep purple foxgloves on my banks to two guests, for whom the flowers and the evening light were good; but gay music not so. And it might, with little pains, have been much otherwise; for if, instead of a somewhat briefly exercised band playing on trumpets and shawms, concerning a Maryland of which they probably did not know, either the place or the history, and an Emperor, a proposal for whose instant expulsion from his dominions would have been probably received with as much applause in the alehouse as the prayer that God would save him upon the lake—if, I say, instead of this tuneful, and occasionally out-of-tuneful, metallic noise, produced with little meaning beyond the noise itself, by the fathers of the village, a few clearly understood and rightly intended words had been chanted for us in harmony by the children of it—suppose, for instance, in truly trained concord and happy understanding, such words as these of Sir Philip Sidney's own, echoed back from the tender ruin of the walls that had been his home, and rising to the fair mountain heaven which is still alike his home and ours:

>"'From snare the fowler lays,
>   He shall thee sure untye;
> The noisome blast that plaguing strays,
>   Untoucht, shall pass thee by.
>"'Soft hived with wing and plume,
>   Thou in his shroud shall lie;
> And on his truth no less presume
>   Than in his shield affy.'

the July sunset would not have been less happy to the little choir, and the peace of it would have been deepened for those to whom it could bring happiness no more.

"'Is any among you afflicted? let him pray; is any merry? let him sing psalms.'

"The entire simplicity and literalness of this command of the first Bishop of the Christian Church cannot, of course, be now believed, in the midst of our luxurious art of the oratorio, and dramatically modulated speeches of Moses in Egypt, and Elijah on Carmel. But the command is, nevertheless, as kind and wise as it is simple; and if ever Old England again becomes Merry England, the first use she will make of her joyful lips will be to sing psalms. I have stated, in the first sketch of the design of our St. George's education, that Music is to be its earliest element, and I think it of so pressing importance to make the required method of musical teaching understood, that I have thrown all other employment aside for the moment, in order to get this edition of Sir Philip Sidney's Psalter prepared for school service.

"I will state the principles of Music and of Song, which it is intended to illustrate as briefly as possible.

"All perfectly rhythmic poetry is meant to be sung to Music, and all entirely noble Music to the illustration of noble words. The art of word and of note, separate from each other, become degraded, and the muse-less sayings, or senseless melodies, harden the intellect or demoralise the ear. Yet better—and manifoldly better—unvocal word and idle note, than the degradation of the most fateful truths of God to be the subjects of scientific piping for our musical pastime. There is excuse, among our uneducated classes, for the Christmas Pantomime, but none, among our educated classes, for the Easter Oratorio.

"The law of nobleness in Music and Poetry is essentially one. Both are the necessary and natural expression of pure and human joy or sorrow, by the lips and fingers of persons trained in right schools to manage their bodies and souls. Every child should be taught, from its youth, to govern its voice discreetly and dexterously, as it does its hands; and not to be able to sing should be more disgraceful than not being able to read or write. For it is quite possible to lead a virtuous and happy life without books or ink, but not without wishing to sing when we are happy, nor without meeting with continual occasions when our song, if right, would be a kind service to others.

"The best Music, like the best Painting, is entirely popular; it at once commends itself to every one, and does so through all ages. The worst Music, like the worst Painting, commends itself at first, in like manner, to ninety-nine people out of a hundred, but after doing them its appointed quantity of mischief, it is forgotten, and new modes of mischief composed. The less we compose at present the better; there is good Music enough written to serve the world for ever; what we want of it for our schools may be gradually gathered under the following general laws of song:

"1. None but beautiful and true words are to be set to Music at all; nor must any be usually sung but those which express the feelings of noble persons under the common circumstances of life, and its actual joys and griefs. Songs extreme in pathos are a morbid form of the indulgence of our desire for excitement; unless in actual dramatic function, becoming part of a great course of thought in which they fulfil the highest tone—as Ophelia's 'White his shroud' which may be properly sung in its appointed place, but there only. It is profane and vulgar to take these pieces out of their shrines; and injurious to all the finer states of thought and habits of life to compose such without shrines.

"2. Accompaniments are always to be subordinate, and the voice of the singer, or choir, supreme. But it is quite possible to keep the richest combinations of instrumental music subordinate to the vocal notes, as great painters can make the richest decoration subordinate to a simple story. And the noblest instrumental execution is felt by true musical instinct to be more conspicuous in this humility and precision of restraint, than in its most consummate dexterity of separate achievement.

"3. Independent instrumental music is to singing what painted glass is to painting; it admits the extremest multiplication, fantasy, range, and concord of note; and has the same functions of magnificence, and powers of awe or pleasure, that the casements have in a cathedral. But all the greatest music is by the human voice, as all greatest painting is of the human face.

"4. All songs are to be sung to their accompaniment, straightforward, as they would be read, or naturally chanted. You must never sing

IV. MUSIC AND EDUCATION.

"'Scots whaw-aw$^{aw}{}^{aW}{}^{aw}$aw-hae wi' Wa-$^{a\text{-}}{}^{a\text{-}}$a-a-$^{a\text{-}}$a-
a-$^{a\text{-}}$a-$^{a\text{-}}$a-$^{a\text{-}}$a-al-lace bled.'

" nor

"'Welcome, welcome, welcome to your go- to your go- to your go-oo-ooo-ory bed;'

"but sing it as you would say it. Neither, even if a song is too short, may you ever extend it by such expedients. You must sing 'Come unto these yellow sands' clear through, and be sorry when it is done; but never

"'Come unto these ya-$^{a\text{-}}{}^{a\text{-}}$a-$^{a\text{-}}$a-$^{a\text{-}}$a- (etc.) -low sands.'

5. The airs of songs by great composers must never be used for other words than those they were written for. Nothing is so destructive of all musical understanding as the habit of fitting a tune that tickles the ear to any syllables

that it will stick on; and a single instance may show the point to which this barbarism has reached in the musical catastrophes of modern concert, prepared for the uneducated and the idle. The other day, on the table of my inn at Cambridge, I chanced to take up a modern 'adaptation' of Rossini's 'Stabat Mater,' and found that the music intended for the Latin syllables, here given in the upper lines, was to be sung indifferently to the English ones below:

> "'Sta-bat Ma-ter Do-lo-ro-sa
> Lord most holy, Lord most migh-ty,
>
> Juxta-ta-Cru-cem La-cry-mo-sa
> Righ-teous ev-er are Thy judg-ments
>
> Dum pen-de-bat Fi-li-us
> Save us, for Thy Mer-cy's sake!'

" Imagine the idea thus conveyed to the listening mob of the composer's intention, or of the dramatic power of his work.

"6. Ballad music is, of course, written with the intent that it shall fit itself to any sentiment by mere difference of adopted time and accent. The right delivery of it will follow naturally on true feeling of the ballad. The absurdity of the ordinary supposition that Music can express feeling definitely, without words, is shown in a moment by the fact that such general expressions *can* be written, and that in any good and classic ballad music, the merry and melancholy parts of the story may be with entire propriety and satisfaction sung to precisely the same melody.

"7. Playful and comic singing are subject to the same laws as play in life and jesting in conversation. No vulgar person can be taught how to play or to jest like a gentleman, and, for the most part, comic songs are for the vulgar only. Their higher standard is fixed, in note and word, by Mozart and Rossini; but I cannot at present judge how far even these men may have lowered the true function of the joyful Muse.

"Thus far of the great general laws under which Music is to be taught in St. George's schools."*

So far the passages quoted have referred to a certain education in Music, which must be present even in its simplest forms if they are to pertain to what may be called the higher ideals, even in simple Music. A passage from the diary of Ruskin's father, shows that a great deal of this manner of thought might almost be considered inherited, at any rate in its germs, notwithstanding the adverse musical conditions of his youth. Mr. Ruskin describes a Swiss family at the Giessbach, singing "Swiss songs in the sweetest and most affecting manner, infinitely

* "Rock Honeycomb," preface.

finer than opera singing, because true alike to Nature and to Music; no grimace nor affectation, nor strained efforts to produce effect." *

Ruskin adds this note: "I shall make this sentence the text of what I have to say, when I have made a few more experiments in our schools here, of the use of Music in peasants' education."

But now, we turn to the education necessary, for appreciation of the higher forms of Music. These Ruskin finds in a much better condition regarding Music, in England, than as regards Painting. He says:

"It is, I believe, as certain that in the last twenty years we have learnt to better understand good Music, and to love it more, as that in the same time our knowledge and love of pictures have not increased. *The reason is easily found. Our Music has been chosen for us by*

* "Dilecta," p. 60.

masters, and our pictures have been chosen by ourselves. If we can imagine exhibitions where good and bad and indifferent symphonies, quartettes, and songs could be heard, not more imperfectly than pictures good, bad, and indifferent are seen at the Academy, and works, to which at a concert we must listen for twenty minutes, were to be listened through in as many seconds, or indeed by an ear glance at a few bars, can we doubt that pretty tunes would be more popular than the finest symphonies of Beethoven, or the loveliest songs of Schubert?"*

Then follows a scheme for doing for Painting what has been done for Music, by the teaching of such men as Charles Hallé, in connection with which, and in comparison with whom, some very

---

* " Fors Clavigera," No. lxxix. p. 194.

IV. MUSIC AND EDUCATION.

scathing remarks are addressed, to such picture dealers as Agnew, who is mentioned by name.

From "Arrows of the Chace" two passages are gathered, one of them perhaps containing one of the earliest expressions of Ruskin's conversion to Music, at any rate as a branch of education. He finds here that Drawing and Music are as necessary to a proper education as writing and arithmetic, but on further consideration fears

"That the cases of physical incapacity of distinguishing sounds would be too frequent to admit of musical knowledge being made a *requirement*." *

This was written in 1857; since when it has been amply proved that incapacity of ear is not sufficiently general to be a drawback in those elementary schools where now Music may be said to be a "requirement;" on the contrary, that it can be remedied to a

* Letter, 1857.

certain extent, for, no doubt, where the Tonic-sol-fa system of teaching intervals prevails, want of ear is to some extent overcome. It is the so-called singing *by* ear, out of tune for generations, which has materially injured the ears of to-day, though they are at present in a hopeful way towards recovery.

The second passage from "Arrows of the Chace" is contained in a letter of 1878, where Mr. Ruskin says :

"I wish I were able to add a few more words with energy and clearness to my former letters, respecting a subject of which my best strength—though in great part lately given to it, has not yet enforced the moment—the function, namely, of the arts of Music and Dancing as leaders and governors of the bodily and instructive mental passions. No nation will ever bring up its youth to be at once refined and pure till its masters have learned the *use* of all the arts and primarily of these. . . . . Let our youth once more learn the meaning of the words music, chorus, and hymns practically; and with the understanding that all such practice, from lowest to highest, is, if rightly done, always in the presence and to the praise of God. . . . . Have you ever heard the charity children sing at St. Paul's? Suppose we sometimes allowed God the honour of seeing our *noble* children collected in right manner to sing to Him, what, think you, might be the effect of such a festival—even if only held once a year—on the national manners and hearts?"*

To many Ruskin students it may appear strange that large extracts are not made here from the "Elements of Prosody," which Mr.

* " Arrows of the Chace."

Ruskin wrote for the purpose of (among other things) "obtaining more direct correspondence between verbal and harmonic intention"; this meant "the note to syllable theory," which has already been referred to in the quotation from "Rock Honeycomb." Mr. Ruskin goes on to say in his preface to "Elements of English Prosody," that all his "musical friends were incredulous or disdainful of the propriety of such a correspondence, and bent unanimously upon establishing a code of abstract sound which should be entirely independent of its meaning." Who these "musical friends" were, I know not, because, in connection with song as a branch of Music, nearly all national song, and many of the finest songs of the greatest song-writers, carry out the theory, virtually, of note to syllable in hundreds of instances. Not of course, will this be found in Handel or the Bellini-Donizetti Italian school, but then one does not look for the "meaning" of Music therein. It has always been the meaning *behind* Music's sound which has attracted Ruskin's thoughts towards it, and our interest in them, and the technical part of his views, treated of in "English Prosody," seems without much meaning in it, or rather, with a meaning which is generally accepted, leaving little or nothing to fight about, and making their statement unnecessary.

A passage of interest must at the same time be extracted from this work as bearing on our subject, though it was perhaps intended to apply more to Poetry, than to Music.

"The strength of poetry is in its thought, not in its form, and with great lyrists, their music is always secondary, and their substance of saying primary (this should be the same in musical sound). So much so that they will even daringly and wilfully leave a syllable or two rough, or even mean, and avoid a perfect rhythm or sweetness, rather than let the reader's mind be drawn away to lean too definitely on the sound."

Would that students took for their text, primarily—"the substance of saying!"

Mr. Ruskin, apart from other theories, wished to prove in "English Prosody" the special varieties of sounds, of which individual forms of verse admit; simply, on account of their individual form. But though he illustrates this musically, and endeavours to arrive at a definite, poetical accent, by means of the different lengths of notes; still nothing of this practical attempt compares with the interest of his words on Music the Ideal. His views of musical technicalities are most untechnical! The ideal, and the spiritual in the art alone, he fathomed; but is not that the Holy of Holies of the Temple? Technicalities have many able exponents, and these matters may be left in their care. The hidden meaning of Music, its inward powers, its educative influences, have very few; and, upon these subjects alone, are Ruskin's words of interest. No man has more fully realised the spiritual essence of art, or given such true expression to its possibilities. In his expression of this, the few will find help and education, but that such teaching can appeal to many is, of course, impossible. General interest, however, cannot be expected, for

'Real music of Doric eagerness, touched of old for the vales and rills, while the still morn went out with sandals grey." *

* " Laws of Fesolé," p. 6.

CHAPTER V.

MUSIC AND MORALS.

"You cannot paint or sing yourselves into being good men. You must be good men before you can either paint or sing, and then the colour and the sound will complete in you all that is best."

Lectures on Art, 1870.

THE foundation of art in moral character is one of the things upon which Ruskin has insisted most forcibly throughout his writings; even those who have followed so far this little collection of his thoughts on Music, must feel, that for him, the full importance of all true art exists, principally, in its moral teaching. So far as it conveys the finest emotions, so far the art is fine; that, which conveys to its hearers base emotions, being no art at all. There is no need to discuss this teaching here; it is familiar to all Ruskin students, and, whether accepted or not, is inseparable from his views on art.

The first passage I find on the subject puts these opinions very distinctly:

"Of course art gift and amiability of disposition are two different things; a good man is not necessarily a painter, nor does an eye for colour necessarily imply an honest mind. But great art implies the union of both powers: it is the expression, by an art gift of a pure soul. If the gift is not there we can have no art at all; and if the soul—and a right soul too—is not there, the art is bad, however dexterous.

But also remember, that the art gift itself is only the result of the moral character of generations. A bad woman may have a sweet voice, but that sweetness of voice comes of the past morality of her race. That she can sing with it at all, she owes to the determination of laws of Music by the morality of the past. Every act, every impulse of virtue and vice, affects in any creature, face, voice, nervous power and vigour and harmony of invention, at once. Perseverance in rightness of human conduct renders, after a certain number of generations, human art possible; every sin clouds it, be it ever so little a one, and persistent vicious living and following of pleasure render, after a certain number of generations, all art impossible. Men are deceived by the long-suffering of the laws of Nature. . . . And for the individual, as soon as you have learned to read, you may, as I said, know him to the heart's core, through his art. Let his art gift be never so cultivated to the height by the schools of a great race of men; it is still but a tapestry thrown over his own being and inner soul."*

"Sesame and Lilies" contains two passages where Music and Morals are closely interwoven in Ruskin's happiest and simplest manner, studiously simple to suit the readers, to whom "Sesame and Lilies" was more especially addressed—the girl-youth of England.

"From the beginning, consider all your accomplishments as means of assistance to others; .... in Music especially you will soon find what personal benefit there is in being serviceable: it is probable that, however limited your powers, you have voice and ear enough to sustain a note of moderate compass in a concerted piece;—that, then, is the first thing to make sure you can do. Get your voice

* "Queen of the Air," pars. 106, 107.

disciplined and clear, and think only of accuracy; never of effect or expression: if you have any soul worth expressing, it will show itself in your singing; but most likely there are very few feelings in you, at present, needing any particular expression; and the one thing you have to do is to make a clear-voiced little instrument of yourself, which other people can entirely depend upon for the note wanted." *

Next must come the passage from "Queen's Gardens," where the necessary things for a girl's moral education are considered.

"Then in art, keep the finest models before her, and let her practice in all her accomplishments to be accurate and thorough, so as to enable her to under-

* "Sesame and Lilies," preface, p. 14.

stand more than she accomplishes. I say the finest models—that is to say, the truest, simplest, usefullest. Note those epithets: they will range through all the arts. Try them in Music, where you might think them the least applicable. I say the truest, that in which the notes most closely and faithfully express the meaning of the words, or the character of intended emotion; again, the simplest, that in which the meaning and melody are attained with the fewest and most significant notes possible; and, finally, the usefullest, that Music which makes the best words most beautiful, which enchants them in our memories each with its own glory of sound, and which applies them closest to the heart at the moment we need them." *

* "Sesame and Lilies," par. 79.

The morals of cradle songs and carols, or rather, those they ought to contain, and why they may not, at present, speak as of old, seem to have occupied Mr. Ruskin's mind in the following passages. Chaucer's carol is reprinted in connection with its context. Finally, Mr. Stuart Mill is credited with producing a terrible un-"Hush-a-by baby-England," with dire results!

"'Hush-a-bye baby, upon the tree top' my mother used to sing to me: and I remember the dawn of intelligence in which I began to object to the bad rhyme which followed :—'when the wind blows the cradle will rock.' But the Christmas winds must blow rudely, and warp the waters askance indeed, which rock our English cradles now.*

"Mendelssohn's songs without words

* "Fors Clavigera," No. xxiv., pp. 19, 20.

have been, I believe, lately popular in musical circles. We shall, perhaps, require cradle songs with very few words, and Christmas carols with very sad ones, before long; in fact, it seems to me, we are fast losing our old skill in carolling. There is a different tone in Chaucer's notion of it (though this carol of his is in spring-time indeed, not at Christmas).

> "'Then went I forth on my right hand,
> Down by a little path I found,
> Of Mintës full and Fennel green.
>
> *   *   *   *
>
> "'Sir Mirth I found, and found anon
> Unto Sir Mirth gan I gone,
> There where he was, him to solace
> And with him, in that happy place,
> So fair folke and so fresh had he,
> That when I saw, I wondered me
> From whence such folk might come,
> So fair were they, all and some;
> For they were like, as in my sight
> To angels, that be feathered bright.
> These folke, of which I tell you so.

"'Upon a karole wenten tho,*
A Ladie karoled them, that hight †
Gladness, blisful and light.
She could make in song such refraining
It sate her wonder well to sing,
Her voice full clear was, and full sweet
She was not rude nor unmeet,
But couth ‡ enough for such doing,
As longeth unto karolling;
For she was wont, in every place,
To singen first, men to solace,
For singing most she gave her to,
No craft had she so lefe § to do."

"Mr. Stuart Mill would have set her to another craft, I fancy (not but that singing is a lucrative one, now-a-days, if it be shrill enough); but you will not get your wives to sing thus for nothing, if you send them out to earn their dinners (instead of earning them yourselves for them), and put their babies summarily to sleep."

* Then.   † Was called.   ‡ Skilful.
§ Fond.   ‖ "Fors Clavigera," No. xxiv. p. 21.

V. MUSIC AND MORALS.

A beautiful passage from Ruskin's third Lecture on Art, may appropriately be introduced here, being almost a summary of his art teaching of Music and Morals.

"Accurately in proportion to the rightness of the cause and the purity of the emotion, is the possibility of the fine art. A maiden may sing of her lost love, but a miser cannot sing of his lost money. And with absolute precision from highest to lowest, *the fineness of the possible art is an index of the moral purity and majesty of the emotion it expresses.* You may test it at any instant. Question with yourselves respecting any feeling that has taken strong possession of your mind, 'Could this be sung by a master, and sung nobly with true melody and art?' Then it is a right feeling. Could it not be sung at all or only sung [ludicrously? It is a base one."*

These passages refer mostly, to the innate moral feeling which exists in the best art. We now come to one touching the artistic morality of the artist, in which, notwithstanding his Mozart worship, Ruskin sees fit to take for his text, on this subject, the librettos of "Zauberflaute" and "Don Giovanni" which he (with many others, though perhaps not for the same reasons) finds "monstrous." These two libretti, are so beneath contempt, in their literary poverty, that it is impossible not to agree with his argument, but when he applies the same artistic moral criticism to "Faust" one feels at issue with him. But, though it is impossible to agree with the passage, most forcibly does it point to his strong feeling, as to the moral effect of art, and to its great importance, as a factor in morals, as well as in education.

* "Lectures on Art," iii.

"Yonder poor horse, calm slave in daily chains at the railroad siding, who drags the detached rear of the train to the front again, and slips aside so deftly as the buffers meet; and, within eighteen inches of death every ten minutes, fulfils his changeless duty all day long, content, for eternal reward, with his night's rest, and his champed mouthful of hay;—anything more earnestly moral and beautiful one cannot imagine—I never see the creature without a kind of worship. And yonder musician, who used the greatest power which (in the art he knew) the Father of Spirits ever yet breathed into the clay of this world;—who used it, I say, to follow and fit with perfect sound the words of the 'Zauberflaute' and of 'Don Giovanni,'—foolishest and most monstrous of conceivable human words and subjects of thought,—

for the future 'amusement' of his race!—No such spectacle of unconscious (and in that unconsciousness all the more fearful) moral degradation of the highest faculty to the lowest purpose can be found in history. But Mozart is nevertheless, a nobler creature than the horse at the siding; nor would it be the least nearer the purpose of his Maker that he, and all his frivolous audiences, should evade the degradation of the profitless piping, only by living, like horses, in daily physical labour for daily bread." *

Later we are told in the same book—

"You do not perhaps know, though I say this diffidently—for I often find working men know many things which one would have thought were out of

---

* "Time and Tide," par. 20.

their way, that Music was among the Greeks, quite the first means of education; and that it was so connected with their system of ethics and of intellectual training, that the God of Music is with them also the God of Righteousness; .... and the Greeks were incontrovertibly right in this. Music is the nearest at hand, the most orderly, the most delicate, and the most perfect of all bodily pleasures, it is also the only one which is equally helpful to all the ages of man,—helpful from the nurse's song to her infant, to the music unheard of others, which so often haunts the deathbed of pure and innocent spirits. And the action of the deceiving or devilish power is in *nothing* shown quite so distinctly among us at this day,—not even in our commercial dishonesties, nor in our social cruelties,—as in its having been able to take away Music, as an instrument of education, altogether; and to enlist it almost wholly in the service of superstition on the one hand, and of sensuality on the other."*

No man has ever been so delightfully inconsistent as Ruskin (who indeed who sees two sides of a question can be otherwise?). The passage that follows from the "Stones of Venice," is a curious contradiction of much he has written, as to the ideal in art being its greatest purpose, which we find elsewhere; but the quotation is interesting, in that it points to a glimmering recognition of Music as Music alone. He says:

"It is at our choice whether we will accompany a poem with Music or not; but if we do the Music *must* be right and neither discordant nor inexpressive.

* "Time and Tide," par. 61.

The goodness and sweetness of the poem cannot save it, if the Music be false; but if the Music be right the poem may be insipid or inharmonious and *still saved by the notes to which it is wedded."* *

It is very true, as an instance of this, that intangible sound has thus preserved for us endless national airs of value, the words of which die, and often deserve to die, even sooner than they do.

By way of contrast to the low level of artistic morality with which he credits some musical works, we shall now see, that Mr. Ruskin finds consolation by returning, in "The Queen of the Air," to some of his beloved Greek myths and philosophy, where Music is the natural expression of a "lofty passion for a right cause."

" In all the loveliest representations in central Greek art of the birth of Athena,

---

* "Stones of Venice," vol. iii. chap. iv.

Apollo stands close to the sitting Jupiter, singing, with a deep, quiet joyfulness to his lyre. The sun is always thought of as the master of time and rhythm, and as the origin of the composing and inventive discovery of melody; but the air, as the actual element and substance of the voice, the prolonging and sustaining power of it, and the symbol of its moral passion. Whatever in Music is measured and designed, belongs therefore to Apollo and the Muses; whatever is impulsive and passionate, to Athena: .... The Apolline Lyre, therefore, is not so much the instrument producing sound, as its measurer and divider by length or tension of string into given notes; and I believe it is in a double connection with its office as a measurer of time or motion, and its relation to the transit of the sun in the sky, that Hermes forms it from the tortoise shell, which is the image of the dappled concave of the cloudy sky. Thenceforward all the limiting or restraining modes of Music belong to the Muses; but the passionate Music is wind Music, as in the Doric flute. Then when this inspired Music becomes degraded in its passion, it sinks to the pipe of Pan, and the double pipe of Marsyas. The myth which represents her doing so is that she invented the double pipe from hearing the hiss of the Gorgonian serpents; but when she played upon it, chancing to see her face reflected in water, she saw it was distorted, whereupon she threw down the flute which Marsyas found. Then the strife of Apollo and Marsyas represents the enduring contest between the Music in which the words and thoughts lead, and the lyre measures or melodises them (which Pindar means when he calls his hymns 'Kings over the Lyre'), and Music in which the words are lost and the wind or impulse leads—generally therefore, between intellectual, and brutal, or meaningless, music. . . . .

"And the opposition of these two kinds of sound is continually dwelt upon by the Greek philosophers, the real fact at the root of all their teaching being this—that true Music is the natural expression of a lofty passion for a right cause; that in proportion to the kingliness and force of any personality, the expression either of its joy or suffering becomes measured, chastened, calm and capable of interpretation only by the majesty of ordered, beautiful, and worded sound. Exactly in proportion to the degree in which we become narrow in the cause and conception of our passions, incontinent in the utterance of them, feeble of perseverance in them, sullied or shameful in the indulgence of them, their expression by musical sound becomes broken, mean, fatuitous, and at last impossible; the measured waves of the air of heaven will not lend themselves to expression of ultimate vice, it must be for ever sunk into discordance or silence. And since, as before stated, every work of right art has a tendency to reproduce the ethical state which first developed it, this, which of all the arts is most distinctly ethical in origin, is also the most direct in power of discipline; the first, the simplest, the most effective of all instruments of moral instruction; while in the failure and betrayal of its functions, it becomes the subtlest aid of moral degradation. Music is thus in her health the teacher of perfect order, and is the voice of the obedience of angels, and the companion of the course of the spheres of heaven; and in her depravity she is also the teacher of perfect disorder and disobedience, and the 'Gloria in Excelsis' becomes the 'Marseillaise.'" . . . .*

" How much of the repose—how much of the wrath, folly and misery of men, has literally depended on this one power of the air—on the sound of the trumpet and of the bell—on the lark's song and the bees' murmur!" †

The extract from " Fors " which follows is given more for the sake of the Music of its words on Music, than for any very direct bearing (which it does not possess) on " Music and Morals." At the same time, the moral element does exist in it, as the whole passage

* " Queen of the Air," pars. 41 & 42.
† *Ibid.*, par. 43.

turns upon the expression of "*noble* thoughts and passions in song."

"The border district of Scotland was at this time, of all districts of the inhabited world, pre-eminently the singing country,—that which most naturally expressed its noble thoughts and passions in song.

"The easily traceable reasons for this character are, I think, the following:

"First, distinctly pastoral life, giving the kind of leisure which, in all ages and countries, solaces itself with simple Music, if other circumstances are favourable—that is to say, if the summer air is mild enough to allow repose, and the race has imagination enough to give motive to verse. . . . .

"Secondly, the soldier's life, passing gradually, not in cowardice or under foreign conquest, but by his own increasing kindness and sense, into that of the shepherd; thus without humiliation leaving the war-wounded past to be recalled for its sorrow and its fame.

"Thirdly, the extreme sadness of that past itself: giving pathos and awe to all the imagery and power of Nature.

"Fourthly (this is a merely physical cause, yet a very notable one), the beauty of the sound of Scottish streams . . . . the pure crystal of the Scottish pebbles, giving the stream its gradations of amber to the edge, and the sound as of 'ravishing division to the Lute,' make the Scottish fords the happiest pieces of all one's day walk. . . . .

"One of the most curious points connected with the study of Border life is this connection of its power of song either with its industry or human love, but never with the religious passion of its

'Independent' mind. The definite subject of the piper or minstrel being always war or love (peasant love as much honoured as the proudest), his feeling is steadily antagonistic to Puritanism; and the discordance of Scottish modern psalmody is as unexampled among civilised nations as the sweetness of their ballads."*

Thus, it will be very plainly perceived, that the word "moral" throughout this chapter must be applied only in its widest art-signification; for the bad art of the Scotch psalm singing (though virtuous!) comes off as badly as the perfect art, misapplied, does in "Don Giovanni!"

A few words must have place here as to an ideal object for use of this much extolled art of song.

"These I say, then, are to be your first

* "Fors Clavigera," No. xxxii. pp. 13–17.

lessons . . . . . the remembrance and honour of the dead with the workmanship for them of fair tombs of song."

Next comes a beautiful account of St. Cecilia and her moral purpose, a study suggested to Ruskin, it seems to me (as, perhaps, were many of his accounts of the Saints, in his "Pleasures of Fancy"), by his minute consideration of his magnificent thirteenth-century musical service book, or antiphonaire. This belonged to, and was originally written for, the Abbesse of Beau Pré. All the music is in the old four-line stave, with the lozenge-shaped notes of the period; but what gorgeous colours, and what wondrous gold, did those thirteenth-century masters shower upon their well-loved vellum. That they fully realised their work was for posterity, is proved by the Latin dedication in this particular volume, which runs to this effect—that to him who makes the charge of this book his special care, it will bring a blessing, but if by chance it falls into the hands of the destroyer

"Anathema" be upon his head! The dedication has guarded the book safely through five centuries, for it is in perfect condition, and those who spent so much beautiful labour on its construction, would feel the aim of their work fulfilled, did they but know the favour it has won, in the eyes of one, who, perhaps in this nineteenth century, stands alone in his power of appreciation of its beauties. I cannot forbear from quoting here a few lines from "Præterita" (though they only bear upon the subject, in so far as Missals contain both "Music and Morals"), in which Mr. Ruskin tells us of his first missal possession, a little fourteenth-century "Hours of the Virgin" acquired by him in 1841. All missals should be his, to whom they can so speak.

"The new worlds which every leaf of this book opened to me and the joy I had counting their letters and unravelling their arabesques, as if they had all been beaten gold—as many of them indeed were—cannot be told. For truly a well illuminated missal is a fairy cathedral, full of painted windows, bound together to carry in one's pocket with the music and the blessing of all its prayers inside."

From the former missal, however, to a certain extent, may have come Ruskin's special interest in the Saint of Song. [The specially beautiful St. Cecilia leaf from it, is reproduced as the frontispiece of this book, though of necessity on a diminished scale.] And now, from this long digression, we return to Ruskin's account of her, who is, at once, the patron Saint, of " Music and Morals."

"With much more clearness and historic comfort we may approach the shrine of St. Cecilia; and even on the most prosaic and realistic minds—such as my own—a visit to her house has a comforting and establishing effect. . . . . The ruling conception of her is deepened gradually by the enlarged study of religious Music; and is at its best and highest in the thirteenth century, when she rather resists than complies with the already tempting and distracting powers of sound, and we are told that 'Cantantibus organis, Cecilia virgo in corde suo soli Domino decantabat, decius, Fiat Domine cor meum et corpus meum immaculatum, ut non confundar.' *

This sentence occurs in my great service book of the Convent of Beau Pré, witten in 1290, and it is illustrated with a miniature of Cecilia sitting silent at a banquet, where all manner of musicians are playing. I need not point out to you how the law, not of sacred Music only so

* Whilst the instruments played, Cecilia the Virgin sang in her heart only to the Lord, saying, "O Lord, be my heart and body made stainless, that she be not confounded."

called but of all Music, is determined by this sentence, which means in effect that unless Music exalt and purify it is not under St. Cecilia's ordinance, and it is not virtually Music at all.

"Her confessed power at last expires amidst a hubbub of odes and sonatas; and I suppose her presence at a Morning Popular is as little anticipated as desired. Unconfessed, she is of all mythic saints the greatest; and the child in its nurse's arms, and every tender and gentle spirit which resolves to purify itself—as the eye for seeing so the ear for hearing—may still, whether behind the temple veil, or at the fireside and by the wayside, hear Cecilia sing."*

Even in this late paragraph comes the technical deficiency, arising from want of musical

---

* "Pleasures of England," iv.

education, which it is impossible not to regret in one, who so understood Music's spiritual essence. For the "Morning Popular" must be allowed to contain, in many ways, the highest of Music's purpose, but still, the voice by the wayside *may* be *the* spiritual version; the Music that lives within Music.

* * * * *

Throughout this little book, apology is necessary, for interposing any ordinary words among those that are of gold; but it is believed that any one, in whom the book may awaken interest, will see in them only their real object, —the desire "to make plain the path," in some instances, perhaps, to translate a hidden thought. Two or three little fragments yet remain which are gathered up, so that nothing may be lost in connection with this subject, though not in two instances, absolutely to be classed under the heading of this chapter.

The first is from the "Laws of Fesolé:"

"Joy and love are not arts, nor are

they limited to humanity. But the love-song becomes art when, by reason and discipline, the singer has become conscious of the ravishment in its divisions to the lute."

Two short sentences from the "Ethics of the Dust" repay thought. The last contains the Music and Moral of Life.

"There is no music in a 'rest' that I know of, but there's the making of Music in it. And people are always missing that part of the life melody, and scrambling on without counting—not that it's easy to count; but nothing on which so much depends ever *is* easy—yet, 'All one's life is a Music, if one touches the notes rightly and in time.'" *

* "Ethics of the Dust."

CHAPTER VI.

CONCLUSION.

OF MUSIC AND "JOANNA'S CARE."

As far as they admitted of classification, the thoughts of "Ruskin on Music" ended in the last chapter, but perhaps, as so often happens, the best of anything does not admit of class selection at all. Such is the case with the passages contained in the following few pages; they touch upon widely differing subjects, but they contain some of the greatest music of words ever sounded.

Of the extracts from "Joanna's Care" (now for the first time separately printed), must it be borne in mind that these beauteous thoughts on Music are probably the last on any subject to which this great mind will ever give expression.

VI. OF MUSIC AND "JOANNA'S CARE."

For those who care specially for the expression of such a mind on an art they love, it is a pleasure to think how near these thoughts have been, and are, to his quiet eventide.

There is a curious significance for Ruskin students even in this limited "Ruskin on Music" selection, that much the largest part of it should relate to what can only be called "Music and Morals." Even in the comparatively small portion of his writings which Ruskin has devoted to Music, the teaching of his life, the insistence on art's moral value and influence, remains its strongest purpose; a value so often ignored, a purpose so often denied to art, and which yet, in the speech of that art, is as the voice of its inner sanctuary; which is to it (in Mr. Ruskin's view) as the Holy Grail to the seekers after Truth.

It is specially pleasant to be able to connect Ruskin's last words on Music with the name of one very dear to him, to whom I have acknowledged my indebtedness, in connection with this little book, in its dedication.

VI. OF MUSIC AND "JOANNA'S CARE."

All the extracts in this chapter are from the number of "Præterita" entitled "Joanna's Care," in which is told a love story of no ordinary interest. A love story indeed, and one of deep and wide significance, but one which has nought to do with the loves of men and maids, which tells of a woman's love for one family, a love which for two generations has been "Faithful unto death," and with which the name of Joan Ruskin Severn must ever be associated.

The words that follow here are, as it were, a summing up of Ruskin's "Thoughts on Music," showing belief in the voice as the eternal musical instrument, in the teaching of all Music to be an eternal service of the highest thought, and its "inner meaning" that which lifts the art to heaven, its inspiration and spiritual essence.

But we must first gather from "Præterita" the passages relating to "Wandering Willie" of "Redgauntlet" fame, to understand all that he suggested to Ruskin in connection with his "prime fiddling," and for a space, it is necessary to look at the context of that which comes more especially under our notice.

Darsie Latimer has escaped from his Quaker friends to the downs of the coast, which had formerly seemed so waste and dreary.

"A moment afterwards he catches the tune of 'Old Sir Thom a Lyne,' sung by three musicians, cosily niched into what you might call a *bunker*,* a little sandpit, dry and snug, surrounded by its banks, and a screen of furze in full bloom. Of whom the youngest, Benjie, at first somewhat dismayed at my appearance, but calculating on my placability, almost in one breath assured the itinerants that I was a grand gentleman, and had plenty of money, and was kind to poor folk, and informed *me* that this

* This is a modern word, meaning, first, a large chest then, a recess scooped in soft rock.

VI. OF MUSIC AND "JOANNA'S CARE." 147

was Willie Steenson, 'Wandering Willie, the best fiddler that ever kittled thairm (catgut) with horsehair.'

"I asked him if he was of this country, '*This* country,' replied the blind man, 'and of every country in broad Scotland, and a wee bit of England to the boot. But yet I am in some sense of this country, *for I was born within hearing of the roar of Solway.*' (Scott.)

"I must pause again to tell the modern reader that no word is ever used by Scott in a hackneyed sense. For three hundred years of English commonplace, *roar* has rhymed to *shore*, as *breeze* to *trees;* yet in this sentence the word is as powerful as if it had never been written till now! for no other sound of the sea is for an instant comparable to the breaking of deep ocean, as it rises over great spaces of sand. In its rise and fall on a rocky coast, it is either perfectly silent, or if it strike, it is with a crash, or a blow like that of a heavy gun. Therefore, under ordinary conditions, there may be either *splash*, or *crash*, or *sigh*, or *boom*, but not *roar*. But the hollow sound of the countless ranks of surfy breakers, rolling mile after mile in ceaseless following, every one of them with the apparent anger and threatening of a fate which is assured death unless fled from,—the sound of this approach over quicksands, and into inextricable gulfs of mountain bay; this, heard far out at sea, or heard far inland, through the peace of secure night,—or stormless day, is still an eternal voice, with the harmony in it of a mighty law, and the gloom of a mortal warning."

No finer, or more musical passage could well be written, than this splendid reference to the eternal voice of Nature's harmony, the root and source of all harmony in art.

Ruskin continues, quoting from Scott:

"The old man preluded as he spoke, and then taking the old tune of 'Galashiels' for his theme, he graced it with a wildness of complicated and beautiful variations, during which it was wonderful to observe how his sightless face was lighted up under the conscious pride and heartfelt delight in the exercise of his own very considerable powers.

"'What think you of that now, for threescore and twa?' (Scott.)

"I pause again to distinguish this noble pride of a man of unerring genius, in the power which all his life has been too short to attain, up to the point he conceives of, from the base complacency of the narrow brain and dull heart, in their own chosen ways of indolence or error.

"The feeling comes out more distinctly still, three pages forward, when his wife tells him, 'The gentleman is a gentleman, Willie; ye maunna speak that gate to him, hinnie?'

"'The deevil I maunna!' said Willie, 'and what for maunna I? If he was ten gentles, he *canna draw a bow like me, can he?*' (Scott.)

"I need to insist upon this distinction, at this time in England especially, when the names of artists, whose birth was an epoch in the world's history, are dragged through the gutters of Paris, Manchester, and New York, to decorate the last puffs written for a morning concert, or a monthly exhibition. I have just turned out of the house a book in which I am told by the modern picture dealer that Mr. A., B., C., D., or F. is 'the Mozart of the nineteenth century'; the fact being that Mozart's birth wrote the laws of melody for all the world as irrevocably as if they had been set down by the waves of Solway; and as widely as the birth of St. Gregory in the sixth century fixed to *its* date for ever the establishment of the laws of musical expression. Men of perfect genius are known in all centuries by their perfect respect to all law, and love of past tradition; their work in the world is never innovation, but new creation, without disturbing for an instant the foundations which were laid of old time."

"Wandering Willie's" notion of the devil as a fiddler, and Ruskin's criticisms on what may be gathered from the passage, follow in rapid succession:

"'Honest folks like me! How do ye ken whether I am honest, or what I am? I may be the deevil himsell for what ye ken: for he has power to come disguised like an angel of light; and besides, he is a prime fiddler. He played a sonata to *Corelli*, ye ken.'

"This reference to the simplest and purest writer of Italian melody being not for the sake of the story, but because Willie's own art had been truly founded upon him, so that he had been really an angel of music as well as light to him. See the beginning of the dialogue in the previous page. 'Do you ken the Laird?' said Willie, interrupting an overture of Corelli, of which he had whistled several bars with great precision.

"I must pause again to crowd together one or two explanations of the references to Music in my own writings hitherto, which I can here sum by asking the reader to compare the use of the voice in war, beginning with the cry of Achilles

VI. OF MUSIC AND "JOANNA'S CARE."

on the Greek wall, down to what may be named as the two great instances of modern choral war-song; the singing of the known Church hymn * at the Battle of Leuthen ('Friedrich,' vol. ii. p. 259), in which 'five-and-twenty thousand victor voices joined:'

> "'Now thank God one and all,
> With heart, with voice, with hands,
> Who wonders great hath done
> To us and to all lands;

and, on the counter side, the song of the 'Marseillaise' on the march to Paris, which began the conquests of the French Revolution, in turning the tide of its enemies. Compare these, I say, with the debased use of modern military bands at dinners and dances, which inaugurate such victory as *we* had at the Battle of

* *Psalm*, I believe, rather; but see my separate notes on "St. Louis's Psalter" (now in preparation).

Balaclava, and the modern no-Battle of the Baltic, when our entire war fleet, a vast job of ironmongers, retreated under Sir C. Napier from before the Russian fortress of Cronstadt.

"I preface with this question the repetition of what I have always taught, that the voice is the eternal musical instrument of heaven and earth, from angels down to birds. Half way between them, my little Joanie sang me yesterday, 13th May, 1889, 'Farewell, Manchester,' and 'Golden Slumbers,' two pieces of consummate melody, which can only be expressed by the voice, and belonging to the group of like melodies which have been, not invented, but inspired, to all nations in the days of their loyalty to God, to their prince, and to themselves. . . . .

"But the distinction of the music of

Scotland from every other is in its association with sweeter natural sounds, and filling a deeper silence. As 'Fors' also ordered it, yesterday afternoon, before Joanie sang these songs to me, I had been, for the first time since my return from Venice, down to the shore of my own lake, with her and her two youngest children, at the little promontory of shingle thrown out into it by the only mountain brook on this eastern side (Beck Leven), which commands the windings of its wooded shore under Furness Fells, and the calm of its fairest expanse of mirror wave—a scene which is in general almost melancholy in its perfect solitude; but when the woods are in their gladness, and the green—how much purer, how much softer than ever emerald!—of their unsullied spring, and the light of dawning summer, possessing alike the clouds and mountains of the west—it is, literally, one of the most beautiful and strange remnants of all that was once most sacred in this British land—all to which we owe, whether the heart, or the voice, of the Douglas 'tender and true,' or the minstrel of the Eildons, or the bard of Plynlimmon, or the Ellen of the lonely Isle,—to whose lips Scott has entrusted the most beautiful Ave Maria that was ever sung, and which can never be sung rightly again until it is remembered that the harp is the true ancient instrument of Scotland as well as of Ireland.*

* Although the violin was known as early as 1270, and occurs again and again in French and Italian sculpture and illumination, its introduction, in superseding both the voice, the golden bell, and the silver trumpet, was entirely owing to the demoralisation of the Spanish kingdom in Naples, of which Evelyn writes in 1644: "The building of the city is, for the size, the most magnificent in Europe. To it belongeth three thousand churches and monasteries, and those best built and adorned of any in Italy. They greatly affect the Spanish gravity in their habit, delight in good

"I am afraid of being diverted too far from Solway Moss, and must ask the reader to look back to my description of the Spirit of Music in the Spanish chapel at Florence ('The Strait Gate,' pages 134 and 135), remembering only this passage at the beginning of it, 'After learning to reason, you will learn to sing: for you will want to. There is much reason for

horses, the streets are full of gallants on horseback, and in coaches and sedans, from hence first brought into England by Sir Sanders Duncomb; the country people so jovial, and addicted to music, that the very husbandmen almost universally play on the guitar, singing and composing songs in praise of their sweethearts, and will commonly go to the field with their fiddle—they are merry, witty, and genial, all which I attribute to the excellent quality of the air."

What Evelyn means by the *fiddle* is not quite certain, since he himself, going to study "in Padua, far beyond the sea," there learned to play on " ye theorba, taught by Signior Dominico Bassano, who had a daughter married to a doctor of laws, that played and sung *to nine* several instruments, with that skill and addresse as few masters in Italy exceeded her; she likewise composed divers excellent pieces. I had never seen any play on the Naples viol before."

singing in the sweet world, when one thinks rightly of it. None for grumbling, provided always you *have* entered in at the strait gate. You will sing all along the road then, in a little while, in a manner pleasant for other people to hear.'"

And so do these thoughts of the "Strait Gate," of Scottish Music and of "Wandering Willie" bring together, as it were, and conclude Ruskin's "meaning" of Music. The humble figure of this man, representative of the true minstrel, being chosen, to record

"for ever the glory—not of Scottish music only, but of all *Music*, rightly so-called—which is a part of God's own creation, becoming an expression of the purest hearts."

Printed by BALLANTYNE, HANSON & CO.
London & Edinburgh.

www.ingramcontent.com/pod-product-compliance
Lightning Source LLC
Chambersburg PA
CBHW030246170426
43202CB00009B/645